D0948745

SLANG OF
THE OPPRESSED
IN AMERICA

TOM DALZELL

DOVER PUBLICATIONS, INC.
Mineola, New York

Bibliographical Note

Damn the Man!: Slang of the Oppressed in America is a new work, first published
by Dover Publications, Inc., in 2010.

Library of Congress Cataloging-in-Publication Data

Dalzell, Tom, 1951–
    Damn the man! : slang of the oppressed in America / Tom Dalzell.
        p. cm.
    Includes bibliographical references and index.
    ISBN-13: 978-0-486-47591-2
    ISBN-10: 0-486-47591-3
    1. English language—Slang. 2. English language—United States—
Rhetoric. 3. Rhetoric—Political aspects—United States. 4. Prejudices—
United States. I. Title.
    PE3711.D35 2010
    417'.2—dc22

                                                                    2010023135

Manufactured in the United States by Courier Corporation
47591301
www.doverpublications.com

❈ ❈ ❈

Lucas: Mitchell's the man, Joe.
Joe: And the man calls all the shots.
Lucas: Damn the man!
  —*Empire Records* (1995)

Acknowledgments

I learned to fight oppression from the best and I thank them, living and gone: the Reverend Alexander McCurdy, Marion Moses, Doug Adair, Hilda Moore, Hope Lopez, Gilbert Padilla, Jerry Cohen, Sandy Nathan, Marshall Ganz, and Jessica Govea. My slang mentors are Madeline Kripke and Paul Dickson. Paul has known *Damn the Man!* as long as I have and placed it with Dover. Stephanie Camp of the University of Washington helped me calibrate the project once I started writing, and her advice was invaluable. Archie Green encouraged and pushed and I hope would be happy.

Contents

Chapter 1

Slang and Oppression

The premise of this book is that in many, but not all, instances, America's oppressed use slang as a gesture of resistance. Slang cannot be used to resist oppression if there is no oppression, which leads to a brief query into the existence of oppression in the United States. The national self-image embraced by many and fueled by politicians on the right does not include historical or contemporary oppression. They tell us that we are, and always have been, exceptional. Through its values, the argument goes, the United States has diverged from the rest of the world and stands above international norms. We are the land of the free, the last best hope for humanity, bearers of the torch of democracy, freedom, and the unleashed human spirit. To even mention oppression is to hate America.

History, of course, teaches otherwise. Alongside our undeniable national achievements stand stark images of oppression—the Middle Passage and slave markets and *Dred Scott*; the Trail of Tears and Wounded Knee; Andrew Carnegie's private army attacking unarmed strikers at Homestead in 1892 and the Colorado National Guard murdering the children and wives of strikers at Ludlow in 1914; the dead immigrant garment workers in the ruins of the Triangle Shirtwaist Factory in 1911; the interment of 120,000 innocent Japanese Americans at Manzanar and Tule Lake and Gila River during World War II; the Zoot Suit riots of 1942–1943 and the police murder of Ruben Salazar during the Chicano

Moratorium in 1970; the McCarthy hearings and Hollywood blacklist of the 1950s; the Edmund Pettus Bridge in 1965 and the Lorraine Motel in 1968 and Klan lynchings; Jim Crow and Wallace and Maddox and Thurmond and Lott; Medgar Evers and James Chaney and Andrew Goodman and Michael Schwerner; People's Park and Kent State and Jackson State; Anita Bryant and Jesse Helms denouncing homosexuals; the murders of Harvey Milk in 1978 and Matthew Shepard in 1998; Rodney King and Amadou Diallo and Abner Louima; and a Constitution that for 133 years denied women the right to vote. In short, we are not without oppression.

To deny our history of oppression is as historically dishonest as it would be to deny our great achievements. Only through conscious and nationalistic ignorance of our failings can we deny that oppression is part of our heritage. A thing of the past? Granted, oppression has in some cases lost its sharpest edges, yet it is a tradition. Isolated or even relatively minor incidents remind and reinforce the relationship between the oppressor and the oppressed in its starkest historical terms.

Oppressed Americans have reacted to oppression just as others elsewhere have always reacted to oppression, somewhere on the spectrum between consent and resistance. Pausing with the notion of a dichotomy of consent and resistance, historian Stephanie Camp makes the brilliant observation that dichotomies obscure as much as they reveal. There are, obviously, reactions to oppression other than the dichotomy of consent and resistance. For example, there are acts of violence between an individual or group members toward another member or group of members of the oppressed group. In *Pedagogy of the Oppressed* (1970), Paulo Freire called this "horizontal violence," and observed the oppressed often "striking out at their own comrades for the pettiest reasons." This lashing out at peers instead of the oppressors is as old as oppression.

Returning to the spectrum and poles, at one pole there are inevitably some who behave in an obsequious and self-degrading manner in the hope of sharing in the privileges of the dominant group. They imagine a nonexistent emotional reciprocity and an illusory identification with their oppressors. They reject resistance and instead elect servility, docility, passivity, ingratiation, subordination, and submission, creating a mimetic, emulative culture that completely accepts the dominant ideals and values. Adaptation, not resistance, is the path these few choose, and theirs is an adaptive culture, not an oppositional culture. Their culture is of no interest when it comes to slang.

While some curry favor with the oppressor, the response to oppression for many has been some degree of resistance—the obstruction, disruption, subversion, or undermining of power by an underdog. The Roman historian Tacitus, who frequently chronicled the Roman Empire's oppression of conquered peoples, wrote, "A desire to resist oppression is implanted in the nature of man." We are, it seems, hard-wired as a species to defy domination.

Henry Highland Garnet, a militant abolitionist, told a group of northern free blacks in 1843, "What kind of resistance you make you must decide by the circumstances that surround you." For some, the resistance made is overt. On the collective level, it may take the form of a brief-lived, heroic, and typically unsuccessful organized, declared, planned uprising—a mutiny, strike, riot, or armed rebellion. On the individual level, it may appear as an act of personal defiance such as desertion, escape, or murder. Harper's Ferry, Nat Turner's revolt, the complex and diverse urban uprisings that began in 1964 in Harlem and continue sporadically into the twenty-first century, the great railroad strike of 1877, the Stonewall riots in 1969, the prisoner revolt at Attica in 1971, and the Weathermen's Days of Rage in 1969 and subsequent bombing campaign are all examples of these intense outbursts of resistance. As glamorous as the thought of razing Babylon may be, the dangers to the oppressed of acting rashly and striking out blindly are many and obvious. In *Rules for Radicals* (1971), Saul Alinsky described these types of resistance as "pointless sure-loser confrontations."

There is a wide range of options, though, between outright defiance and obsequious consent. James Scott wrote in *Domination and the Arts of Resistance* (1990), "Most of the political life of subordinate groups is to be found neither in overt collective defiance of powerholders nor in complete hegemonic compliance, but in the vast territory between these two polar opposites." The underclass, underdogs, outcasts, outlaws, outsiders, disenfranchised, and powerless who resist oppression, exploitation, discrimination, and humiliation in some form short of violent resistance are the great, not-silent majority. Scott went further in

Weapons of the Weak, arguing that when multiplied, these small acts of everyday resistance "may in the end make utter shambles of the policies dreamed up by their would-be superiors."

There are many weapons for those who choose resistance short of rebellion that require no planning or coordination. James Scott calls these acts Brechtian resistance; others simply call them acts of everyday resistance or indirect expressions of dissent. These tiny acts of rebellion are less dramatic and less daring and less romantic, yet more common and more successful than overt, organized resistance. Behaviors that in the words of John W. Roberts in *From Trickster to Badman* (1989), "circumvented the master's power rather than directly challenging it" are most often the most effective, and certainly the safest forms of resistance.

Everyday resistance is often seen in subtle acts of passive aggression, including feigning illness, malingering, shirking work, foot-dragging, cheating, self-inflicted injury, avoidance, tardiness, pretending to misunderstand orders, insolence, exaggerated compliance to the point of mockery, mumbling, grumbling, evasive tactics, and deliberate negligence such as tool-breaking.

Another set of resistance behaviors are based on disguise. Affected ignorance, naiveté, simplicity, pretense, rituals of reversal such as carnival symbolism, and grins and lies enable resistance from behind a mask of public compliance.

Resistance can also be seen in acts of public anonymity that shield the identity of the actors. Rumor, gossip, graffiti, anonymous threats, conjuration, spirit possession, and magic all serve the oppressed in their everyday resistance by undermining the authority, supremacy, and invincibility of the oppressor.

Slightly bolder are actions that approach but do not reach the level of overt defiance. Cheating, lying, petty theft, spontaneous acts of arson or sabotage, and poaching all deceive and subvert the authority of the oppressor without the risks of open revolt.

Lastly, expressive culture offers the oppressed a means to circumvent rather than directly challenge the oppressor. Religion, music, folktale, and dress all serve as forms of everyday resistance. Religion and folktales are used to express a desire for liberation without explicitly advocating secular resistance. To be sure, religion can also divert resistance. As Marx's "sigh of the oppressed creature," religion can be seen as the opiate of the masses. On the other hand, in religion the oppressed cannot only find solace, they can express quiet and acceptable dissent through Biblical or religious metaphors of liberation. Similarly, seemingly harmless folktales, jokes, songs, and poems about small and weak animals who through quick-thinking outwit and defeat bigger and stronger animals once served as a safe challenge to the authority of the oppressor.

To the oppressed, distinctive clothing styles sometimes serve as "an emphatic repudiation of their allotted social role," to borrow a phrase from White et al, *Stylin'* (1998). Music, too, can express resistance indirectly. Revolutionary theorist Frantz Fanon wrote that without oppression and racism there could have been no blues, and he predicted that the end of racism "would sound the knell of great Negro music," just as Hugh Masekala predicted that the great music of South Africa's townships would end with the end of apartheid. Spirituals with their message of liberation, secular work songs representing mass activity when mass activity was prohibited, and the blues or "devil music" all served slaves and then freemen as outlets of resistance. Through the blues, jazz, rhythm and blues, and hip-hop, American blacks have dissented.

Slang lies within this general category of defiant expressive culture.

Even absent any political context, slang tests the boundaries of standard language. It represents linguistic defiance and, at times, linguistic rebellion. James Sledd wrote a short and brilliant article about slang, "On Not Teaching English Usage" in *The English Journal* (November 1965), stating "Slang serves the outs as a weapon against the ins. To use slang is to deny allegiance to the existing order, either jokingly or in earnest, by refusing even the words which represent convention and signal status; and those who are paid to preserve the status quo are prompted to repress slang as they are prompted to repress any other symbol of potential revolution."

Thus it has always been. On a grand scale, colonists resisting England forged American English as a gesture of resistance. Noah Webster explicitly argued that America had its own language, manifested in spelling, definitions, and usage that set America apart from England. If perversion of standard British English by the colonists was not bad enough, American slang of the late eighteenth and early nineteenth century further registered dissent. In the ditty "Yankee Doodle Dandy," Americans embraced the British view of them as simpletons (a "doodle" meant a simpleton), ridiculed upper-class British styles by comparing a feather in the cap to stylish Italian hairstyles favored by London's elite (the "macaroni"), and impudently ridiculed British soldiers as "lobster backs." Members of the American Continental Army who wintered at Valley Forge grumbled about their food, which they called "fire cakes," proving that even those who are oppressed within a revolutionary movement use slang to strike out at life's vicissitudes.

The oppressed in America have been great manufacturers and distributors of new language. Language, especially slang, plays a key role in cultures of resistance. Those who are oppressed by the dominant culture or by an authoritarian institution that controls their lives manifest through their language their creative nature and the spirit of resistance. While slang is not always subversive, when employed by an underclass or underculture it can be a witty, humorous, and effective gesture of resistance. It is no accident that the liveliest language in America is often the product of the ghetto, *shtetl*, slum, *barrio*, barracks, and prison yards.

The oppressed create and use slang to build individual and group identity, to separate themselves from the dominant culture. This separation, with its distinct values and ethics, is critically important for the identity and survival of the oppressed group. With slang as oppositional culture, the dominated compensate for oppression, exploitation, discrimination, and humiliation. Slang becomes for the oppressed an outward and physical manifestation of a subversive refusal to be subservient. Slang evolves from a covert expression of independence and identity ("I am one of us") to an overt expression of group strength. Those who make resistance engage in a political bricolage, using whatever materials happen to be available—in this case, language.

Language is used by the oppressed to a limited degree to hide the meaning of their speech from the dominant culture, but more importantly, to reinforce the identity of the culture in the face of domination by the ascendant culture. It is laced with an anti-authoritarian sentiment, a linguistic rage against the machine. The slang of the oppressed rings with distrust, anger, and resistance. Slang becomes a language of liberation.

As is shown in the chapters that follow, common threads found in the idiom of many oppressed groups include:

1. Construction of a collective identity, communal values, and solidarity. Slang alone does not create an "us," but it reinforces a sense of solidarity.
2. Inversion and incongruity, or the world upside down. Good is bad, and bad is good. In the counter-narrative of the oppressed, the outlaw is often the admired archetype. The language of the oppressed supports this sense of insurgency.
3. Scorn for the oppressor. Alinsky wrote in *Rules for Radicals* (1971), "Ridicule is man's most potent weapon," and ridicule and absurdity abound in the slang of the oppressed, helping unmask the oppressor.
4. A robust vocabulary demonstrating hatred for those among the oppressed class who side with the oppressor.
5. A sense of respect for each other absent in daily life. For example, in a world where whites commonly referred to blacks as "boy," black hipsters made a fetish of calling each other "man."
6. Humor, creativity, and double meaning that allow communication with a freedom denied in other forms of expression.
7. Strong words, hyperbole, and deliberate vulgarity.

Not all oppressed groups use slang, Lesbians, for instance, do not have a grand slang lexicon, largely because of the ties between lesbians and the women's movement. Similarly, Asian Americans are undeniably oppressed, yet their language is lacking, if not bereft, of slang because standard English and the linguistic norms of middle-class white America are keys to the upward mobility which they desire.

Further, not all members of slang-using oppressed groups use slang. Further yet, not all use of slang by members of oppressed groups is intended as a gesture of resistance. At times, slang is simply imitative. It is also used purely for its joy and aesthetic, poetic value. Actions interpreted for some as resistance to oppression should not be interpreted as resistance for all.

Enough theory—time to stop living on our knees and instead to prepare to die on our feet, for today is a good day to die—let's live free or die! Whistling "Bridge Over the River Kwai," let's show them what happens when they tread on us, let's tear down the walls, serve the people, bring the war home, and take a sister by the hand, far away from this foreign land! The whole world is watching—and—we're not going to take it—and—*el pueblo unido jamas sera vencido!* Hell no, we won't go! All power to the people! Free Bobby, Free Huey! Burn, baby, burn! Fan the flames of discontent! Total resistance! *VIVA LA HUELGA!* No Justice, No Peace! Kick out the jams, motherfucker—and—we don't need a weatherman to know which way the wind blows—so—Damn the Man!—rage against the machine—no retreat, no surrender. What does that spell? What does that spell? What does that spell . . . .

CHAPTER 2

African Americans

Africans Americans are as logical a group as any to serve as a starting point in a discussion of oppression in America. Yes, others have been harshly oppressed. The conquest and near genocide of Native American Indians and the suppression of all women as less than political and economic equals represent brutal and debilitating oppression. African Americans, though, were brought here as chattel, stripped of their native languages and identities, and even when freed from slavery were subjected to systematic denial of human rights, social equality, civil rights, and equal economic opportunity. For good reason it is the African American who is the icon of oppression in American culture, illustrated by the titles of Jerry Farber's *The Student as Nigger*, Jane Gallion's *The Woman as Nigger*, and Raymond Parrish's *The Veteran as Nigger*.

Despite—or is it because of—this oppression, for much of the twentieth century, black culture has driven mainstream American popular culture, from music to fashion to sports to language. It can be argued convincingly that since the late 1930s, black vernacular English has shaped American slang to a greater degree than any other influence. From the jive jargon of jazz musicians in the 1930s to the keep-it-real slang of today's hip-hop culture, the language of African Americans is bright and profoundly subversive. Entire books have been and will be written about African-American English; the focus here will be on the relationship between oppression and black language.

The Language of Slaves

Slave traders and American enslavers quickly stripped slaves of their native languages. Beginning on the slave ships that brought Africans to the New World and continuing onto the plantations of the South, slaves were methodically separated from other speakers of their native language to prevent possible uprisings during the crossing of the Atlantic or on plantations. Revolutionary theorist Paolo Freire in *Pedagogy of the Oppressed* (1970) observed that oppressors inhibit the creativity of the oppressed "by curbing their expression." So it was here, where enslavers in the New World planned the disappearance of African languages. African languages surely survived in the New World for a time, but not for long. As native languages were driven from memory, even hollow-log drums were outlawed for fear that they would be used to broadcast sedition.

The obliteration of native African languages left slaves without national identities. All other immigrants to the United States have brought with them some sense of national identity rooted in language, music, food, and custom. Mexican and Filipino immigrants, like Italians and other Europeans who came before them, maintain a home-village identity in the United States. The Filipino immigrant even has a word for a fellow townsman, the Tagalog word *kababayan*, and fraternal organizations based on hometowns in the Philippine Islands are still found in California's San Joaquin Valley. African slaves, on the other hand, were without a country and for all intents and purposes without a past.

Without their native languages, slaves had to improvise immediately to communicate. It may be that the Senegalese language Wolof was briefly used as a *linga franca* in some places in the colonies, but to the extent that it was, it was not used for long. Throughout the slave-holding colonies, an English-based pidgin—a language of transaction without any native speakers—soon developed, providing slaves with a first line of defense against the oppression of slavery in a strange land. Over time, the pidgin acquired native speakers in new generations and thus evolved into a creole.

Enslavers ruthlessly punished any slave who dared to try to learn to read or write, leaving the spoken word as the only form of lexical communication. This supported the oral linguistic traditions of Africa and reinforced in black Americans an oral-aural world that has persisted.

Evolution: Creole to Vernacular to Urban Jive

By the early 1800s, legal importation of slaves to the new United States had ended. Through time, American-born slaves came to dominate the slave population. As their African roots faded and they became more American, the slave Creole gradually lost much of its African structural features and evolved toward English as spoken by white Americans, although not without the African pidgin heritage.

The pidgin and Creole of slaves and then freed slaves was highly coded, with meanings hidden from whites, and this tradition persisted through Emancipation and into the twentieth century migration of southern blacks to northern cities. In the 1920s and 1930s, African-American vernacular took a giant leap forward as it evolved from rural to urban. New Orleans, Chicago, and Harlem were the breeding grounds for an explosive growth in black slang, fueled by the counter-insurgency of jazz. As they fought to establish and defend a distinctly black musical idiom, black jazz musicians were prolific in coining slang to describe their music, lives, and values. White jazz musicians of the 1940s and then white disc jockeys of the 1950s and 1960s helped transplant black urban slang into white America, but there was a through-story in black ghettos—slang was passed from generation to generation in a natural and organic way, with new coinings added to the mix. When hip-hop burst onto the scene in the 1980s, large parts of the "new" hip-hop lexicon could be traced directly to the lexicon of the 1930s black jazz musician.

Slang was not the only linguistic weapon of oppressed blacks. Also in the quiver was "fancy talk," oratorical splendor that strayed from standard English in the opposite boundary from slang. Slang, though, has been the language weapon of choice. Clarence Major, a noted scholar of African-American language, characterizes it as "a natural attempt to counteract the classic and dreary weight of political and social oppression" in his *Dictionary of Afro-American Slang* (1970). Major went further—"Black slang stems more precisely from a somewhat disseminated rejection of the life-styles, social patterns, and thinking in general of the Euro-American sensibility." Newspaper writer and early Harlem jive connoisseur Dan Burley observed likewise in *Handbook for Harlem Jive* (1946) that slang is "A safety valve of people pressed against the wall for centuries."

As is the case in the vernacular of other oppressed groups, slang in the black community not only softened the impact of white oppression, it obscured and enabled resistance to that oppression. In the terminology of semanticist Alfred Korzybski, African-American slang is not just the map, it is also the territory. Beyond the literal meaning of the words (the map) is a powerful message of resistance (the territory).

R-E-S-P-E-C-T

One universal response to oppression is for the oppressed to construct a collective identity with counter-cultural communal values and a sense of solidarity. Often, slang is one of the building blocks for this brave new identity that is not defined by the oppressor. To be sure, slang alone does not create an "us," but it can and does reflect and reinforce a sense of solidarity. Thus it has been with African Americans.

Clarence Major wrote in *Dictionary of Afro-American Slang* (1970) that black vernacular "is a language unconsciously designed to pave a way toward positive self-images." In even stronger language, he asserted, "the sociocultural factors at the root of it are revolutionary." Similarly, Geneva Smitherman, a linguist at Michigan State University and author of *Talkin and Testifyin* (1977), wrote that slang "has allowed blacks to create a culture of survival in an alien land."

In slang, African Americans found a key attribute missing in their daily interactions with whites—respect. When Republican Congressman Geoff Davis of Kentucky called soon-to-be President Barack Obama "boy" in April 2008, he tapped into, intentionally or not, a long tradition of oppressive racism. After centuries of being called "boy," "mammy," "uncle," or worse, it is not surprising that an early feature of African-American English was the bestowing of respect where respect had been denied. Historians Shane and Graham White studied the balls and parades put on by northern blacks in the late nineteenth century and in *Stylin'* (1998) observed "They universally address each other by the titles of Mr., Mrs., Miss, Sir, and Madam."

Fast-forward to the 1930s and listen to the vernacular of urban black hipsters, and you will find, in the words of Robin Kelley in *Race Rebels* (1994), that they "made a fetish of calling each other 'man'" This echoes an earlier observation from *Monthly Review* cited by Robert Gold in *A Jazz Lexicon* (1957): "Negroes habitually call each other 'man' in reaction to a lifetime of being addressed by white folk as 'boy.'" Similarly, Malachi Andrew described **man** in *Black Talk* (1973) as "a term used to counter the force of the rhetoric of boy." As an aside, the use of royal honorifics in nicknames such as Count Basie and Duke Ellington was no accident.

As a term of address used in greeting, **man** (1568) is ubiquitous in African-American vernacular.

⠿ ⠿ ⠿

Aw, **man**, you ain't willing to go very far."
—Zora Neale Hurston: *"Story in Harlem Slang,"*
American Mercury (July 1942) 91

"I said, 'Hey, **man**, how you doin'?" He said, "Oh, I'm doin' fine, Sonny."
—Claude Brown: *Manchild in the Promised Land*
(1965) 225

In addition to supplying respect where it had been lacking, **man** served a second function without any hint of resistance. As observed in the *Daily Colonist* on April 16, 1959, it "saves cool cat hangup of remembering names."

If the goal is to construct a new, positive self-identity, what better metaphor to adopt than that of the family? Drawing on the family, in black vernacular an African-American woman is a **sister** or **soul sister**, and an African-American man is, yes, a **brother** or **soul brother**.

Although **soul sister** (1967) was recorded before the simpler **sister** (1968), **sister** meaning a black woman soon drove the longer original from the field.

⠿ ⠿ ⠿

Sitting up on the customer's seat was a big fine **sister**
who was popping her fingers and wiggling to the music
and smiling at me because our eyes had met.
—Eldridge Cleaver: *Soul on Ice* (1968) 28

But O.J. had the "good-looking man" factor going for
him. Those middle-aged **sisters** came to court every day
and stared at this good-looking man they'd like to fuck.
　　　—Chris Rock: *Rock This!* (1997) 204

I've also noticed that most of our **soul sisters**, they
marry whitey.
　　　—Babs Gonzales: *Movin' On Down De Line*
　　　(1975) 54

For undetermined reasons, **soul sister** was never widely accepted; August Meier in *The Making of Black America* (1969) characterized **soul sister** as less common than **soul brother**.

Brother (1910) was not a term coined in the sixties, but in the sixties
black militants latched onto it to mean a black man, and the term never
looked back.

※ ※ ※

Young bloods wanted to be like these **brothers**.
　　　—H. Rap Brown: *Die Nigger Die!* (1969) 15

And if we got some righteous work to do for black
liberation, whether it's with guns or if it's just recruiting
brothers who are interested, then let's get it on!
　　　—Bobby Seale: *A Lonely Rage* (1978) 170

As was the case with **soul sister** and **sister**, **soul brother** (1959) never
attained the popularity of the simpler **brother**.

※ ※ ※

A certain **Soul Brother** passing by took out his heat
and shot both of them bastards.
　　　—Babs Gonzales: *Movin' On Down De Line*
　　　(1975) 54

SOUL BROTHER—A Black MAN moving in Blackness.
　　　—Malachi Andrews: *Black Talk* (1973) 62

I say that if you throws that thing, I'm gonna have
myself one **soul brother** in heaven!
> —Robert Conot: *Rivers of Blood, Years of Darkness*
> (1967) 302

Family is sometimes referred as "blood," as in "blood relative," and this link, or the essential role of blood in life, explains the use of **young blood** (1946) to refer, especially as a term of address, to a younger African-American man, and then the widespread use of **blood** (1965) to refer to any African American.

⚃ ⚃ ⚃

Does all this sound like I'm making it up, **youngblood**?
> —Eldridge Cleaver: *Soul on Ice* (1968) 160

Now **Youngblood**, about Pepper. You don't know
anything about her.
> —Iceberg Slim: *Pimp* (1969) 66

"I wouldn't jive you, **youngblood**," he answered his
critic with a deadpan under his cap.
> —Odie Hawkins: *The Busting Out of an*
> *Ordinary Man* (1985) 88

Annette downtown going for broke, while Chicanos
and **bloods** outside the bars beat the nightlight out of
po' trash from across the way, driving them out of their
territory.
> —Steve Cannon: *Groove, Bang, and Jive Around*
> (1969) 24

They never inquired if the **bloods** they were giving
the jobs to were the same ones who were causing the
trouble.
> —Tom Wolfe: *Radical Chic & Mau-Mauing*
> *the Flak Catchers* (1970) 98–99

The rise of the Bloods youth gang in Los Angeles in the mid-1970s may have diminished use of the word for fear of suggesting an allegiance that is best unsuggested, but the term certainly had its day.

Leaving the family, black vernacular builds community with a reference to community. **Homeboy** (1899), **homegirl** (1934), and **homey** or **homie** (1944) all define a fellow African American in terms of a shared neighborhood. The neighborhood may be literal—a city block—or it may be figurative—the African-American community as a whole seen as a metaphorical neighborhood.

⁑ ⁑ ⁑

"My **homeboy**! Man, gimme some skin! I'm from Lansing."
>—Malcolm X: *The Autobiography of Malcolm X* (1964) 44

"You my **homeboy**, and the dude who ain't from around here, he ain't one of us."
>—H. Rap Brown: *Die Nigger Die!* (1969) 16

You really playin with power there, **homegirl**!
>—Jess Mowry: *Way Past Cool* (1992) 28

I just called my **homegirl**, Amber, just before you got here, and she was talkin' crazy about how she was gonna kill herself and how I should get her funeral clothes together.
>—*Rolling Stone* (April 12, 2001) 80

Dragging along some of his Washington **homies**, including 1 special loudmouth named Barry Gusey.
>—Clarence Cooper: *The Farm* (1967) 87

That's my lady **homey**. Her name's Brandi.
>—"Boyz 'N the Hood" (1990)

Called up the **homies** and I'm askin' y'all / Which park are y'all playing basketball?
>—Ice Cube: "It Was a Good Day" (1993)

And then there is the queen of all African-American bonding terms, **soul**, both as a noun (1946), meaning the quintessence, spirit, and core of black culture, and as an adjective (1946). Roger Abrahams captured the heart of soul in *Positively Black* (1970): "The use of 'soul' in black parlance drives in this same direction, toward a sense of ethnic unity based on an innate, irrational sense of community, brotherhood."

⠿ ⠿ ⠿

"Man, what can anybody see in a gray chick, when colored chicks are so fine; they got so much **soul**." This was the coming of the "soul" thing too.
　　—Claude Brown: *Manchild in the Promised Land*
　　(1965) 172

The AAA gave "**Soul** Parties." Everyone greeting with the new handshake, doing African dances that looked like overexaggerated gyrations.
　　—Bobby Seale: *A Lonely Rage* (1978) 164

Related terms used to capture a sense of cultural solidarity include **soul music** (1961), **soul food** (1964), and **Soulville** (1975), referring to a predominantly black neighborhood.

⠿ ⠿ ⠿

Soul music *n.* uniquely black music composed by black musicians, which transmits much of the culture and feeling of blackness.
　　—David Claerbaut: *Black Jargon in White America*
　　(1972) 80

"**Soul**" music was important not just as a musical idiom, but also as a black-defined, black-accepted means of *actively* involving the mass base of Negroes. It was, in fact, the "self-definition" Stokely Carmichael was to call for later through cultural action rather than verbalized terms.
　　—Ben Sidran: *Black Talk* (1971) 126

The emphasis on **Soul Food** is counter-revolutionary
black bourgeois ideology.
 —Eldridge Cleaver: *Soul on Ice* (1968) 29

We don't even have our own food. **Soul food** is not
black food. It's some nasty shit they fed to the slaves.
You think a ham hock tasted good the first time the
white man shoved it in our faces? No.
 —Chris Rock: *Rock This!* (1997) 13

He hired me to gig for him after I closed in **soulville** so
we just moved downtown to whitey-ville for six more
weeks.
 —Babs Gonzales: *Movin' On Down De Line*
 (1975) 33

The need for self-defined affirmation can also be seen in the use of
word up! (1986) or **word!** (1987) to convey agreement or assent. The
suggestion of solidarity is clear—within our people, nothing more than
a person's word is needed.

⠶ ⠶ ⠶

Rac nodded. "**Word up**! By rules!"
 —Jess Mowry: *Way Past Cool* (1992) 13

But now, **word**! Hey, I be selling thirty-forty caps in a
few minutes.
 —Terry Williams: *The Cocaine Kids* (1989) 57

"**Word**" was once a powerful affirmation that you were
"dropping science" [making sense].
 —Nelson George: *Hip Hop America* (1998) 209

Lastly, there is the vocabulary of everyday acts of resistance. One
act of everyday resistance that is common to many oppressed peoples
is intentional tardiness or, at least, a decided lack of punctuality. This
weapon was and is used by African Americans, who even in an era when

"colored people" is hopelessly outdated still recognize and use **colored people's time** (1925) or the abbreviated **CPT** or the half-abbreviated **CP time**.

⁑ ⁑ ⁑

> **CPT—Colored People's Time** (i.e., on time when they WANT to be, otherwise NOT).
> > —San Francisco Chronicle (May 9, 1967) 33

> And come on time, not **C.P.T**.
> > —Letter from Langston Hughes to
> > Carl Van Vechten (September 23, 1949)

> In recognition of the fact that a stereotype as developed regarding **C.P. Time**, the first 15 minutes of any meeting shall henceforth be known as J.T. (Jive Time).
> > —Carolyn Greene: *70 Soul Secrets of Sapphire*
> > (1973)

> **C.P.T.—Colored People Time**—Late. A Black person subconsciously releases generations of pressure provoked by white society (i.e., creates more of his freedom) by getting there "Whenever I gets ready to be there."
> > —Malachi Andrews: *Black Talk* (1973) 91

> If you made an appointment with one of them, you couldn't bring them any slow **cp (colored people's) time**.
> > —Ralph Ellison: *Invisible Man* (1952) 163

Derivatives applied to other ethnicities abound—**Indian time** (1963) **Jewish people's time** or **JPT** (1967), **Mexican time** (1967), **Chicano time** (1972), and **Alaska time** (1976). From New Zealand comes **Maori time** (2002) and from Trinidad comes **Trinidad time** and **Trini time** (1990). Conversely, Native American students were recorded using **white man's time** (1963) for conveying disgust of their punctuality.

Another form of everyday resistance is found in expressive culture, such as insider handshakes and hairstyles. With these manifestations of expressive culture as resistance came a vernacular. In the hairstyle department, there was the bushy style of the late 1960s and the 1970s, known as an **Afro** (1966), **'Fro** (1970), or **natural** (1969), and the **pick** (1982) used to comb it.

※ ※ ※

I knew everything about O.J. from reading that 90-page book that third graders could order from the Weekly Reader. I remember knowing that he had a fine wife and an **Afro**.
—Chris Rock: *Rock This!* (1997) 206

I don't know how anybody could've recognized us, you especially with that **'fro**.
—Elmore Leonard: *Freaky Deaky* (1988) 35

Some with fluffy **naturals** like my sister Angie, some with silky **naturals** like my sister Betty.
—George Jackson: *Soledad Brother* (1970) 313

Her once scrawny frame was all softness and curves, and she looked like an African princess, with her hair in a then uncommon **Natural**.
—Iceberg Slim: *The Naked Soul of Iceberg Slim* (1971) 83

He pulled out his hair **pick** and fluffed up his **'fro**.
—John Del Vecchio: *Thirteenth Valley* (1982) 130

In later decades, Afrocentric hairstyles favored tight braids arranged in rows delineated by bare scalp, or **corn rows** (1946).

✖ ✖ ✖

After several trips to Africa he decided to give up his "natural" and wear what the black brothers call "**corn rows**."
    —*San Francisco Chronicle* (June 5, 1972) 54

Sapphire knows how to **corn-row** hair.
    —Carolyn Greene: *70 Soul Secrets of Sapphire*
      (1973) 25

With the vocabulary of resistance through expressive culture came a vocabulary for consent through expressive culture. Chemical or heat straightened hair was known as a **conk** (1942) with a verb form to **conk** (1942).

✖ ✖ ✖

He'd drop by the school and be vined down. He was clean. Had him a **conk** then and he knew he was ready.
    —H. Rap Brown: *Die Nigger Die!* (1969) 24

Some of them look like, you know, with the fancy hair [referring to high **conks** or "process," straightened and teased hair].
    —Christina and Richard Milner: *Black Players*
      (1972) 114

The face of a colored youth with slick **conked** hair and beardless cheeks stared up.
    —Chester Himes: *The Real Cool Killers* (1959) 25

Everybody understood that my head had to stay kinky a while longer, to grow long enough for Shorty to **conk** it for me.
    —Malcolm X: *The Autobiography of Malcolm X*
      (1964) 51

Last but not least is the vocabulary of the expressive culture of identity-affirming handshakes. In the beginning was **giving five** (1935), the mutual slapping of palms.

░░ ░░ ░░

Murphy leaned forward to **give** his partner **five**. "Right on, brother! Right on!"
—Odie Hawkins: *Chicago Hustle* (1977) 98–99

I had it because a week later Chillie **gave me five** [a stylized hand slap] and the coke was in his hand.
—Terry Williams: *The Cocaine Kids* (1989) 78

Well into its life span, **give me five** got an energy boost from **high five** (1980), a ritualistic slapping of the palms shoulder-high or higher.

░░ ░░ ░░

Nikki gave me a **high five**. "Play on, playa."
—Zane: *Chocolate Flava* (2004) 83

The woof chorus went through the roof, everybody **high-fiving**, bopping in glee.
—Richard Price: *Clockers* (1992) 205

After **giving five** came **skin** (1942) and to **give skin** (1964), ritualistic palm-to-palm contact as a greeting or affirmation.

░░ ░░ ░░

"What is it, my man," he yelled out as he came up and held his hand out for some **skin**.
—Donald Goines: *Cry Revenge* (1974) 101

He nearly dropped the powder can. "My homeboy! Man, **gimme some skin**! I'm from Lansing."
—Malcolm X: *The Autobiography of Malcolm X* (1964) 44

Proving that slang never sleeps, along came **dap** as a noun (1972) and a verb (1973), referring to any of many rituals of hand greetings, especially among African-American soldiers in Vietnam.

⚒ ⚒ ⚒

Race consciousness took the form of symbolic cultural behavior, for example, involved handshakes or the "**dap**."
—Charles Figley: *Strangers at Home* (1980) 79

Even if you just hate my fuckin guts go 'head and **dap** me / Cause I'm gon' **dap** you anyway and then go home and pray for yo' ass later.
—Outkast: "Wailin'" (1996)

The World Upside Down

Central to any resistance or liberation canon is the belief that one day the first shall be last and the last shall be first. If this sentiment sounds vaguely familiar, it is perhaps because this is the central theme of the Sermon on the Mount ("Blessed are the poor in spirit . . .")—or, perhaps, because of Acts 17:6 ("These that have turned the world upside down are come hither also")—or perhaps, because of Dylan's lyrics in "The Times They Are A-Changin'" ("And the loser now, will later to win . . .") or perhaps—probably not, but perhaps—because of the seventeenth-century anti-Cromwell ballad "The World Turned Upside Down" ("Let's be content, and the times lament, you see the world turn'd upside down").

This inversion or turning of the world upside down has been a prime feature of African-American popular culture. In many African-American jokes, the normal relationship between blacks and whites is suddenly reversed and the absurd comedy of inverting the roles unmasks and humiliates the oppressor. Similarly, in the animal folktales of the nineteenth century and the narrative poems of the twentieth century, the smaller and weaker animal—B'rer Rabbit or Anansi or the Signifying Monkey—outwits and triumphs over the larger and stronger animal. As Eithne Quinn observed in *Nuthin' but a 'G' Thang* (2005), much of the fashion sense of contemporary African-American youth can be seen in terms of the world upside down. Prison garb—baggy jeans, no belt, denim, and head rags—are embraced as a fashion statement, inversion if ever there was inversion.

So too for African-American slang. A prominent feature of black vernacular is a linguistic world-upside-down view, in that what the dominant society views as positive is negative, and vice-versa. There are many examples of this phenomenon, but an examination of three seminal examples—**bad**, **cool**, and **square**—illustrates the point well.

Bad (1897) meaning "good" is as good—or is it bad?—a place to start in the bad-is-good-and-good-is-bad corner. The early attestations are not African American, but at least by the 1950s the usage was fully ensconced in African-American slang. On October 11, 1955, the *Philadelphia Evening Bulletin* explained the inversion to its readers:

> The latest bop talk requires you to say, if you like a musician, "Man, he's real **bad**." Or, "he blows **bad**." This critical pronouncement, delivered in a monotone, with the "b-a-a-d" dragged out for emphasis, means the exact opposite of what it says.

Claude Brown also felt it necessary to explain in *Manchild in the Promised Land* (1965) this reversal of roles and poles:

> In this day, when somebody would say someone was a **bad** cat, they meant that he was good. Somebody would say, "That was some **bad** pot, meaning it was good."

Even in 1973, Malachi Andrews felt compelled to explain the world upside down in his didactic *Black Talk:*

> **BAD**—Here the black man has taken a word that the white man has used to depict him and made it into a word that describes the beautiful elements of his own life.

One final example, by Malcolm X in his *Autobiography* (1964), illustrates the use of **bad** as admirable in a tough sense.

> "I've mentioned him before—one of Harlem's really **bad** Negroes."

With **bad**, slang mirrors the evolution of folklore, where the wily trickster who dominated African-American popular culture in the nineteenth century had graduated by the early twentieth century to a tough, dominating bully in the mold of Stagolee, a new, tougher archetype of resistance.

In a world where **bad** is good, the best—or toughest and most admired—is not the correct "worst" but the more poetic **baddest** (1938).

❇ ❇ ❇

Some folks say that Willie Green / was the **baddest**
motherfucker the world ever seen."
    —Bruce Jackson: *Get Your Ass in the Water and*
      Swim Like Me (1970) 57

Yeah though I walk through the valley of death, I shall
fear no evil, 'cause I'm the **baddest** motherfucker in the
valley."
    —Wallace Terry: *Bloods* (1984) 243

"Anything that happens, this nigger's the **baddest**
nigger you ever seen."
    —Bobby Seale: *Seize the Time* (1991) 92

While still in the **bad** department, there are several common compounds, such as **bad motherfucker** (1964), applied to a fearless tough person.

❇ ❇ ❇

Said the signifying monkey to the lion that very same
day / "There's a **bad motherfucker** heading your way."
    —Bruce Jackson: *Get Your Ass in the Water and*
      Swim Like Me (1970) 57

Right then and there I knew the **bad motherfucker** was
playin' the dozens."
    —William Labov: *A Study of the Non-Standard*
      English of Negro and Puerto Rican Speakers (1968) 90

I'm a **bad motherfucker** / Rap the rip-saw, the devil's
brother-in-law.
> —H. Rap Brown: *Die Nigger Die!* (1969) 28

I'm known as a **bad motherfucker**.
> —Roger Abrahams: *Deep Down in the Jungle*
> (1964) 131

There is no more memorable **bad motherfucker** moment than Jules
(Samuel L. Jackson) in *Pulp Fiction* explaining to the bumbling restaurant
robbers that his wallet was the one that said "**bad motherfucker**."

Also used by African-American speakers as praise is **bad nigger**
(1965), a staggering combination of inversion and appropriation of a
hate-word.

⠿ ⠿ ⠿

I learned that a **bad nigger** was a nigger who didn't
take no shit from nobody and that even the "crackers"
didn't mess with him.
> —Claude Brown: *Manchild in the Promised Land*
> (1965) 47

Slightly less provocative is **bad ass** (1956), a tough person who does not
know fear.

⠿ ⠿ ⠿

Now Dolomite went on down to Kansas City / kickin'
asses till both shoes were shitty / Hoboed into Chi /
Who did he run into but that **badass** Two-Gun Pete.
> —Bruce Jackson: *Get Your Ass in the Water and*
> *Swim Like Me* (1970) 59

Just then you could hear a pin drop, for that **bad-ass**
Benny Long walked in the door.
> —Roger Abrahams: *Deep Down in the Jungle*
> (1964) 131

As an adjective, **bad-ass** (1955) conveys the same admiration for toughness that the noun ascribes.

※ ※ ※

I told him about hanging out with those **bad-ass** boys.
—Claude Brown: *Manchild in the Promised Land*
(1965) 10

Now down on the ground in a great big ring / Lived a
bad-ass lion who knew he was king.
—Dennis Wepman: *The Life* (1976) 22

"Man, that's about one **bad ass** nigger," a voice came
from the crowd.
—Joseph Nazel: *Black Cop* (1993) 63

The swap of **hot** to **cool** to mean good is a complicated story that can be oversimplified as follows: (1) **hot** (1845) meant excellent and later had a specific application to jazz (1918); (2) **cool** (1933) began to be used by African Americans to mean excellent and later had a specific application to jazz (1948); and (3) **cool** rapidly became the all-time number-one slang term for good throughout the general population of the United States. In a world upside down, what was **hot** became, naturally, **cool**.

This narrative is complicated because not all data fits into a nicely wrapped package with ribbon and bow. The first pure attestation of **cool** as excellent was in 1933:

※ ※ ※

"And his mouf is jes' crammed full of gold teeth. Sho
wisht it wuz mine. And whut make it so **cool**, he got
money'cumulated."
—Zora Neale Hurston: "Spunk" (1933) in *The
Complete Stories* (1995) 26

The Oxford English Dictionary has gathered a number of examples of **cool kind daddy** and **cool kind mama** starting in 1924, precise meaning not included, but there is no further evidence, as of this writing, of a pure **cool** until the lyrics of a 1947 Cab Calloway song, and then in the late 1940s and early 1950s the floodgates let loose. This surge of **cool** as excellent coincided with the birth of **cool** in the jazz sense. First recorded in this sense in 1948, the term came into its own in the next several years. The different streams of cool—a jazz style, stylish, and excellent—muddy the waters, but the basic flow is sound. The last shall be first, and the hot shall be cool.

There is no better example of good-is-bad than the reversal of **square** that took place in Harlem in the late 1930s. For centuries, to call someone **square** meant, to borrow definitions from the Oxford English Dictionary, that they were "solid, steady, reliable" (1589) or "honest or straightforward in dealing with others" (1646).

In the world upside down of African-American slang, a **square** (1939) became a person who was naïve to a fault and profoundly out of touch with current style and tastes. The earliest attestation, uncovered by Stephen Goarson of Duke University's library system, is from a Harlem glossary:

⠿ ⠿ ⠿

> **Square**. A bore, pest (syn: jeff, icky). After all, a square often deserves to be Igged.
> —"American Slang," *Punch* (March 15, 1939)
> 283

Benjamin Zimmer is not far behind, finding a second 1939 usage in the *New York Amsterdam News*:

⠿ ⠿ ⠿

> Lawd! I'm a **square** from Delaware, a Lane from Spokane, a killer from Manila and a Home from Rome.
> —Dan Burley: "Backdoor Stuff" in *New York Amsterdam News* (May 27, 1939) 20

In the same year, Cab Calloway issued a small dictionary of jive for new converts to swing jazz, in which he proclaimed:

❖ ❖ ❖

Square: an un-hip person.
   —Cab Calloway: *The New Cab Calloway's Cat-Ologue* (1939)

The term, on its own and embellished as **square from Delaware**, was quickly and wildly popular.

❖ ❖ ❖

A lot of the guys who hung around were **squares** who worked for their gold, more gamblers than gangsters.
   —Mezz Mezzrow: *Really the Blues* (1946) 20

'Coz the good times is over / And the **squares** don't have no dough.
   —Jimmy Witherspoon: "Skid Row Blues" (1947)

I had out-slicked the law / and taken off a whole lotta **squares**.
   —Lightnin' Rod (Jalal Nuriddin): *Hustlers Convention* (1973) 29

Square (1946) also appears as an adjective denoting a lack of awareness.

❖ ❖ ❖

You won't find it in the **square**-nigger or white history books.
   —Iceberg Slim: *Pimp* (1969) 194

They can tell pimps from **square** guys. They can tell
square girls from prostitutes.
—Susan Hall: *Gentlemen of Leisure* (1972) 4

They would prefer that he date a ho or **square** broad.
—Christina and Richard Milner: *Black Players*
(1973) 72

Scorn for the Oppressor

The slang of African Americans is bursting with a lexicon of contempt
for their oppressors. After centuries of slavery, Jim Crow, benign neglect,
deindustrialization, and poverty, it should not be surprising that their
slang became a cultural repository for ridicule, scorn, hostility, disdain,
and contempt for white oppressors.

After being defined by their white oppressors on the basis of their skin
color for centuries, African Americans understandably have a number of
derisive terms for white people that draw upon, well, the color of their
skin. **Whitey** (1942) is the prototype. While it was a favorite of militants,
less-than-militant African-American writers used the term effortlessly.

❊ ❊ ❊

So **whitey** would get him a little taste of black gold for
$10 or $15.
—H. Rap Brown: *Die Nigger Die!* (1969) 31

And then I got to see how **Whitey** treats his heroes.
—Dick Gregory: *Nigger* (1964) 72

Shorty felt about the war the same way I and most
ghetto Negroes did: "**Whitey** owns everything. He
wants us to go and bleed for him? Let him fight.
—Malcolm X: *Autobiography of Malcolm X* (1964) 71

In 1939 Negroes were still relegated to sitting in the
balconies of downtown theatres so we decided to
change "**whitey's**" rule.
—Babs Gonzales: *I Paid My Dues* (1967) 14

White trash (1822) refers to poor rural whites. Mezz Mezzrow, a white jazz musician who spent his life working and associating with African Americans, used the term with the proper degree of contempt:

⠿ ⠿ ⠿

> When good old Buck, of Buck and Bubbles, was driving along down South in his big Cadillac and dared to challenge the supremacy of the white race by passing a couple of **white trash** in a dinky old rattletrap Ford, he spent the night in jail.
> —Mezz Mezzrow: *Really the Blues* (1946) 207

In the article "Caddy Buffers—Legends of a Middle-Class Negro Family in Philadelphia" included by Alan Dundes in *Mother Wit from the Laughing Barrel* (1990), Kathryn Morgan writes, "She would spend hours telling them how to get even with the **white trash** that talked about niggers."

White meat (1957) is used to describe a white person as a purely sexual object.

⠿ ⠿ ⠿

> "Shoot, whyn't they try to get them some nice **white meat** from downtown once in a while instead of picking on us all the time?"
> —John Murtagh and Sara Harris: *Cast the First Stone* (1957) 111

Continuing into the minor leagues with the white theme are **chalk** (1945), the lovely metaphor **fishbelly** (1986), and **snowball**, recorded in *Maledicta*, Volume IV, Number 1 (1980) by Laurence French.

⠿ ⠿ ⠿

> "If it wasn't for Uncle Tom ass dudes like me, niggers like you wouldn't be havin' a chance to eat all the **chalk** pussy you want."
> —Odie Hawkins: *Chicago Hustle* (1977) 138

He was with this skinny **chalk** who was rapping on
'bout how dope kills young kids.
>—Shane Stevens: *Way Uptown* (1971) 33

"You go on back to Boston, **fishbelly**, and stay there
and don't come near my lady again."
>—Robert Parker: *Taming a Seahorse* (1986) 39

While at the light end of the street, there is **pink** (1926) and **pink toes**
(1980).

⠶ ⠶ ⠶

"Funny thing about those **pink**-chasers, the ofays never
seem to have any use for them."
>—Carl Van Vechten: *Nigger Heaven* (1926) 157

"Was she that big Gawga **pink** work as a tacker?"
Pigmeat asked.
>—Chester Himes: *If He Hollers Let Him Go*
>   (1945) 103

In no time at all Konky got on the ball / And had ten
whores—nine **pinks** and a shade."
>—Dennis Wepman: *The Life* (1976) 103

Geneva Smitherman writes in *Talkin and Testifyin* (1977) of **pink toes** as
referring to white women, alluding to "the supposed softness and ten-
derness of their feet."

Last but not least in the color department is the etymologically enig-
matic **gray** (1944), which folklore linguist Roger Abrahams in *Positively
Black* (1970) called "for a time, the most common term for whites in Negro parlance," and the related **gray boy** (1951) and **gray broad** (1966).
Abrahams argues the intuitive, that gray diminished the black/white
dichotomy and drove white people from the "good" pole. Malachi Andrews agreed in *Black Talk* (1973): "This word is a comeback to the racist
system which was afraid that the freedom of Black people would turn the
world into GRAY." Ken Johnson, collected in Thomas Kochman's *Rappin'
and Stylin' Out* (1972), argues that the term "implies the 'dead' nature

of white people in their physical appearance and actions." Still others suggest a link to the color of the uniform of the regular forces of the Confederate Army. Whatever the origin, it was used with contempt.

❖ ❖ ❖

I doubt that they're many, if any, **gray** people who
could ever say "baby" to a negro.
>—Claude Brown: *Manchild in the Promised Land*
>(1965) 266

Leaving the pale descriptors, African Americans have referred to whites as simply **the devil** (1980) or the embellished **blue-eyed devil** (1964). Malcolm X branded **blue-eyed devil** and others picked up:

❖ ❖ ❖

The **blue-eyed devil** has twisted his Christianity, to
keep his foot on our backs.
>—Malcolm X: *Autobiography of Malcom X*
>(1964) 205

The **blue-eyed devil** is in trouble.
>—Harry Edwards (speaking of the black power
>salute that American runners Tommie Smith
>and John Carlos gave at the 1968 Olympics
>in Mexico City) in Amy Bass: *Not the Triumph
>but the Struggle* (1968) 197

"I'm tellin' you I know what that **blue-eyed devil** has
hooked you up on."
>—Odie Hawkins: *Ghetto Sketches* (1972) 210

Edith Folb, a leading expert on African-American vernacular, included the simpler **devil** in her 1980 glossary *Runnin' Down Some Lines* and termed it "especially derogatory."

A final epitome-of-evil term for whites is **Babylonian** (2004), recorded at Berkeley High School, Berkeley, California, by David Ayers in

Berkeley High Slang Dictionary. **Babylon** was used first in Jamaica (1943) to mean the white power structure or the police, and as such became a significant player in the Rastafarian vocabulary according to F.G. Cassidy and R.B. LePage in *Dictionary of Jamaican English* (1967). David Claerbaut recorded the term in an early black vernacular English lexicon *Black Jargon in White America* (1972) as meaning the United States, a usage supported twenty years later.

⠶ ⠶ ⠶

> Black people came also to see the white people
> increasingly clearly as their oppressors and the white
> (or near-white) establishment as "**Babylon**."
> —Alrick Cambridge: *Where You Belong* (1992) 60

Of the several personifications of the white man, none is more common than **Mister Charlie** (1928).

⠶ ⠶ ⠶

> He talks about **Mister Charlie** and he says he's with
> us—us kids—but he ain't going to do nothing to offend
> him.
> —James Baldwin: *Blues for Mister Charlie* (1964) 40

> Goldberg's just as bad as **Mr. Charlie**.
> —Claude Brown: *Manchild in the Promised Land*
> (1965) 295

> "**Mr. Charlie, Mr. Charlie**. Who the fuck is he?"
> "That's the name Brew calls the paddies."
> —Piri Thomas: *Down These Mean Streets* (1967) 145

> Pretty soon it's gonna be all over for **Mr. Charlie**.
> —Nathan McCall: *Makes Me Wanna Holler*
> (1995) 100

Variations on the theme include **Big Charlie** (1968), **Charlie** (1928), **Charlene** (1972), **Chuck** (1965), **Jeff** (1959), an evolution of an earlier meaning (1938)—a stupid man—and a display of obvious and overt contempt for Jefferson Davis and the Confederacy.

⊞ ⊞ ⊞

I knows they's nothing but overseers on the big
plantation, jes doin like **Big Charlie** tell 'em to.
   —Robert Gover: *JC Saves* (1968) 112

I am perplexed and hard pressed in finding a solution
or reason that will adequately explain why we are so
eager to follow **Charlie**.
   —George Jackson: *Soledad Brother* (1965) 67

Sapphire is the world's foremost authority on **Charlie**.
She has borne his children, been his servant, his
mistress, his confidante, and the recipient of perversion
for hundreds of years.
   —Carolyn Green: *70 Soul Secrets of Sapphire*
    (1973) 32

Charlene: the feminine version of "Mr. Charlie."
   —Ken Johnson in Thomas Kochman: *Rappin'*
    and Stylin' Out (1972) 144

That's the same thing that **Mr. Chuck's** been doing all
these years.
   —Claude Brown: *Manchild in the Promised Land*
    (1965) 333

"It went from "white man" to "whitey," from "Mr.
Charlie" to "**Chuck**."
   —Julius Lester: *Watch Out Whitey!* (1968) 19

Chalk the walking **Jeffs**.
   —Chester Himes: *The Real Cool Killers* (1959) 120

Jeff, n. A white person, but esp. one who is hostile to
Negroes.
　　　　—Robert Gold: *A Jazz Lexicon* (1964) 165

Miss Ann or **Missy Ann** (1925) is the most popular politely contemptuous term for a white woman.

⠶ ⠶ ⠶

"Well, **Miss Anne**," he said, "if we both got the same
thing on our mind, let's make it to that party."
　　　　—James Baldwin: *Another Country* (1961) 121

This, **Miss Ann** of the Clansman and Rev. Dixon's
finest dream, here in whose name thousands of
blackthroats have been stretched and a million
blackballs crushed.
　　　　—Clarence Cooper: *The Farm* (1967) 25–26

Is he gonna grow up t'be a bid bad see-eye-aye man an
keep the word safe fo' **Missy Ann's** fur coat?
　　　　—Robert Gover: *JC Saves* (1968) 70

Other central terms in the African-American slang lexicon are **buckra,
cracker, honkey, ofay, paddy,** and **peckerwood.**

Buckra (1787) is as old as the hills, with an undoubtedly African origin
(meaning either "master" or "devil"), although authorities do not agree
on exactly what African language. It is a term that was more frequently
heard in the eighteenth century, but it is still occasionally heard today.

⠶ ⠶ ⠶

Not to mention **buckra** bitches accusing you of rape.
　　　　—John Brunner: *The Stone That Never
　　　　Came Down* (1973) 56

Cracker (1766) is a prized pejorative with an unsettled etymology. Many argue that it is an abbreviated "corn-cracker," but not all agree, pointing to the earlier sense of the word meaning a braggart or, improbably in the case of an etymology offered by Malachi Andrews in *Black Talk* (1973), "from the whip cracked over Black People." The word suggests a white person with a southern heritage, a lack of education, and overt racism.

⚏ ⚏ ⚏

Hell, I'm from Arkansas where the **crackers** lynch
niggers in the street.
  —Langston Hughes: *Ways of White Folks* (1934) 62

I was working down the aisle and a big, beefy, red-
faced **cracker** soldier got up in front of me.
  —Malcolm X: *Autobiography of Malcolm X*
    (1964) 77

I think we ought to just challenge for the heck of it
every two hours or so, just to let those **crackers** know
that we are on our toes and they'd better not try
anything.
  —Stokely Carmichael: *Black Power* (1967) 110

They went out to the highway and caught a ride with a
young **cracker** in a '55 Ford.
  —Cecil Brown: *The Life and Loves of Mr. Jiveass
    Nigger* (1969) 27

The ever-popular **honky** (1958) evolved from the earlier **hunky** (1909), which was used to refer to Eastern Europeans, especially Slavs. The most popular cute but false etymology, repeated by Malachi Andrews in *Black Talk* (1973) among others, is that **honky** came because white people who had driven to pick up their black servants would honk their horns from the curb rather than walk to the servant's door. If it weren't for Hungary, there would be no **honky**.

※ ※ ※

They couldn't care less about the old, stiffassed **honkies**
who don't like their new dances.
　　　—Eldridge Cleaver: *Soul on Ice* (1968) 81

You come back here and kill one racist, red-necked
honkey camel-breathed peckerwood who's been
misusing you and your people all your life and that's
murder.
　　　—H. Rap Brown: *Die Nigger Die!* (1969) 38

Ironically, **hunky** (1959) later came full circle and emerged as a sub-
stitute for **honky** to deride whites.

※ ※ ※

He said, "I'm going to buy this building and turn this
into a Nigger bar. I'm going to bar all you laughing
hunkies."
　　　—Iceberg Slim: *Trick Baby* (1970) 149

Dem **Hunkies** couldn't care less if a nigger was born on
Mars.
　　　—J. Ashton Brathwaite: *Niggers—This is Canada*
　　　(1971) 24

Even more ironically, Jonathan Lighter records two instances of the word
as applied to a black person, dated 1928 and 1980.

Ofay (1925) is a special word, if only because of the deep divisions
in theories about its origin. The popular but almost certainly incorrect
theory is that it was formed as Pig Latin for "foe." Slang etymologist
Gerald Cohen argues that it is a corruption of the French *au fait*, which
means up to date. The *Dictionary of American Regional English* points to
the Ibibio language of Nigeria. Whatever its etymology, **ofay** has many
advocates.

⬛ ⬛ ⬛

It was a pleasure house, where those rich **ofay** (white)
business men and planters would come from all
over the South and spend some awful large amounts
of loot.
    —Louis Armstrong: *Satchmo* (1954) 147

"I don't know the names of all the **ofays** who come
into my place."
    —Chester Himes: *The Real Cool Killers* (1959) 63

My father was away fighting for the land of the **Ofay**.
    —H. Rap Brown: *Die Nigger Die!* (1969) 42

"You one of those **ofay** liberals who's got high hopes."
    —Nathan Heard: *Howard Street* (1968) 151

Jazz musician Mezz Mezzrow used the variant **ofaginzy** (1946), which
was colorful but probably not widely used:

⬛ ⬛ ⬛

"May why don't you come clean, don't nobody
fault you for makin' out you's **ofaginzy**,' talking as
though he was on the girls' side and knew I was
really colored."
    —Mezz Mezzrow: *Really the Blues* (1946) 204

Paddy (1945) had been used as a diminutive of "Patrick" to mean an
Irishman since 1780, but in the mid-1940s it began to be used to mean
a white man (1945) and a policeman (1946). The suggestion in *Black
Talk* (1973) by Malachi Andrews that **paddy** comes from **patty** because
white people had a habit of "patting Negroes on the head, back and ass
all the time" is silly. The Irish invented **paddy**.

> "Hey, don't spit in the sink where you wash the glasses," some **paddy** down the bar said.
> —Chester Himes: *Black on Black I* (1946) 256

> "We ought to beat the hell out of those **paddies**!
> —Ralph Ellison: *The Invisible Man* (1947) 268

> I told this **paddy** and solemnly did swear / no more farm for me—too damn many ups out there.
> —Bruce Jackson: *Get Your Ass in the Water* (1966) 198

Borrowing from **peckerwood** *(below)*, there is the infrequent **paddy wood** (1980) collected in Philadelphia by Edith Folb in *Runnin' Down Some Lines* (1980).

Peckerwood (1904) is the last major contestant in the scorn-whites-in-general-as-oppressors category. The earlier sense (1859) of the word was a woodpecker morphed by reversing the syllables; the human association is rural and bigoted, not bird-related.

> And, man, you ain't seen a **peckerwood** until you've seen Lyle Britten.
> —James Baldwin: *Blues for Mister Charlie* (1964) 40

> And Grandma told me what **peckerwoods** were.
> —Claude Brown: *Manchild in the Promised Land* (1965) 48

> Did you know that **peckerwood** of Pepper's is the bankroll behind the biggest policy wheel in town?
> —Iceberg Slim: *Pimp* (1969) 67

Peckerwood variants include the predictable **peck** (1924) and the unpredictable **featherwood** (1989) for a white woman.

‭‬‭‬‭‬ ‭‬‭‬‭‬ ‭‬‭‬‭‬

Of course, a poor white **peck** will cuss. A poor white
peck will cuss worse'n a nigger.
　　　—Cecil Brown: *The Life and Loves of Mr. Jiveass*
　　　Nigger (1969) 6

With prison slang recorded in *A Convict's Dictionary* (1989) by James
Harris, **featherwood** starts with **peckerwood**, treats **pecker** as meaning
penis, drops **pecker** and adds **feather** (soft female pubic hair).

　Finally, infrequently recorded terms of scorn for whites include **fade**
(1972) recorded as prison slang by Bentley and Corbett in *Prison Slang*
(1969), **keebler** (1992) gathered by Terry Williams from crack cocaine
addicts in *Crackhouse* (1992), **maggot** (1985) as recorded in New York
by Carsten Stroud in *Close Pursuit* (1987), **neck** (1966), a shortened "red-
neck" recorded as prison slang in *Dictionary of Desperation* (1976) by John
Armore, and **rabbit** (1991) recorded as Vietnam war slang by Linda
Reinberg in *In The Field* (1991) and as prison slang by Gary Farlow in
Prison-ese (2002).

　Whatever disdain black Americans may have for racist whites in general pales in comparison to the disdain felt for white racist police, the
type of men who would refer to their baton as a **nigger stick** (1971) or as
black-on-black crime as **NHI** (meaning "no humans involved") (1971).
Pig (1811) is the all-time number one term used for police, especially
white police, in the African-American vernacular. The term was first
recorded in the United Kingdom in 1811, but it was the Black Panthers
who pushed the term to the top of the charts in the 1960s. The Panthers' official publication frequently used the term, defining a **pig** as "an
ill-natured beast who has no respect for law and order, a foul traducer
who's usually found masquerading as a victim of an unprovoked attack."
The Black Panther (May 1967). Others spat the word in contempt:

‭‬‭‬‭‬ ‭‬‭‬‭‬ ‭‬‭‬‭‬

I escaped from Kern County jail and fought the **pigs**, all
the way back to the midwestern area of my birth.
　　　—George Jackson: *Soledad Brother* (1970) 41

A **pig** was downed, another wounded with numerous
shots.
  —Bobby Seale: *A Lonely Rage* (1978) 225

The term produced variants such as **porker** (1998) and the anti-police
chant of the 1960s—"Today's pig, tomorrow's bacon."
 Another epithet for police that is used by but not coined by African
Americans is **fuzz** (1929). While there are several popular explanations
for the origin of the term, those who know these things agree that they
don't know the origin.

⠶ ⠶ ⠶

All of us was taking off a joint, and the **fuzz** busted
down on us and shot Dirty Red and Tim.
  —Donald Goines: *Dopefiend* (1971) 154

The **fuzz** told his partner that it was just a family beef.
  —A. S. Jackson: *Gentleman Pimp* (1973) 152

The man (1928) expresses less contempt than **pig**, but is not used
kindly when used to mean the police.

⠶ ⠶ ⠶

"You're **the man**, ain't you?" "Yeah, I'm **the man**."
  —Chester Himes: *The Real Cool Killers* (1959)

You just had to keep watching for **the Man**. He was
always looking for cats who were down there jostling.
  —Claude Brown: *Manchild in the Promised Land*
  (1965) 160–161

"I thought maybe you was **the man**. Them cats work
on Sundays too."
  —Piri Thomas: *Down These Mean Streets* (1967) 328

The term is frequently used in a broader sense to mean the entire dominant white, oppressive establishment. In a similar vein is **the Law** (1893), coined by others but occasionally used by African Americans.

:: :: ::

> The men grumble and reluctantly spread themselves
> along the wall, prodded by **the Law**.
> —Odie Hawkins: *Ghetto Sketches* (972) 31

> So **the laws** heard the shots.
> —Bruce Jackson: *The Life* (1976) 66

Other examples of slang terms for police used by African Americans include **five-o** (1983), **jake** recorded in New York by Carsten Stroud in *Close Pursuit* (1987), the verb-turned-noun **nab** (1813) and **po-lice** (1972).

:: :: ::

> "Yo! Yo! You **5-0**. This dude is a cop!"
> —*New Jack City* (1990)

> He couldn't afford to have "**Nab**" [police] catch
> anything in his short.
> —Babs Gonzales: *I Paid My Dues* (1967) 98

> Still, it took about six months before we had learned
> to talk enough "game" to earn their respect as non-
> squares, and for suspicions that we might be "**po-lice**"
> to evaporate.
> —Christina and Richard Milner: *Black Players*
>   (1972) 24

Code warnings that police are near include **one-time!** (1992), **po-po!** (1990), and **slick boys!** (1991).

※ ※ ※

"**One-time**! Break!"
    —*Menace II Society* (1992)

The cop call—**Po-Po**—was a neighborly warning
sounded by whoever spotted the police for anyone who
might like to know.
    —Adrian LeBlanc: *Random Family* (2003) 107

The windows of the car were open, and the two men
could hear children in the neighborhood yell "**Slick boys!**"
    —*Chicago Tribune* (January 9, 1991) C1

One police presence that announces itself and needs no warning is the
police helicopter, or **ghetto bird**.

※ ※ ※

Police and media helicopters, known in south-central
Los Angeles as **ghetto birds**, saw nothing by calm.
    —*CNN News* (April 17, 1993)

Edith Folb collected a number of additional pieces of slang-for-police
from black teenagers in Philadelphia in 1980—**Charlie Irvine**, **divine
right**, **do-right**, **gray dog**, **J. Edgar**, **Johnny-be-good**, **Junior Walker**,
Peter Jay, and **Sherlock Holmes.**
    Jews were scorned by urban African Americans in the era when Jew-
ish merchants dominated commerce in black ghettos. **Goldberg** (1965)
was the most consistently used pejorative.

※ ※ ※

This was the first time I'd ever heard "**Goldberg**" used
this way. I said, "Who's **Goldberg**?" "You now, Mr. Jew.
That's the cat who runs the garment center."
    —Claude Brown: *Manchild in the Promised Land*
    (1965) 295

Finally, scorn is poured upon whites who embrace the mannerisms and affectations of their African-American peers, everything black but the burden, in the words of Greg Tate. Since the white minstrel shows of the early 19th centuries, whites have posed as blacks while expropriating black culture. The practice waited for many years until **wannabe** (1980). **Wannabe** has broader meaning, but it was first recorded by Edith Folb in use by black teenagers in Philadelphia and in a 1985 article:

✄ ✄ ✄

They call the white gangs "**wannabes**," meaning someone who dresses and talks the part because he "wants to be" a gang member, but is actually tame.
—*Los Angeles Times* (July 28, 1985) Metro
Section 4

Whatever its broader meaning has become, **wannabe** started life as a term used to demean white posers.

Wigger (1988)—a contraction of "white" + "nigger" is the best of show when it comes to contempt for white people affecting black mannerisms. White rapper Marshall Mathers placed the word in context in a self-reflecting song:

✄ ✄ ✄

These cocky Caucasians / Who think I'm some **wigger** who just tries to be black / 'Cuz I talk with an accent.
—Marshall Mathers: *The Way I Am* (2000)

The vocabulary used by whites to describe African Americans over the years is impressive, but no less impressive is the vocabulary used by African Americans to describe their white oppressors. Words do hurt, and with slang blacks hurt back.

Siding with the Oppressor

To the oppressed, there is a special vitriol reserved for those who seek to advance their own interests by consenting to oppression. The 1931 coal miner song "Which Side Are You On?" is a powerful articulation that in certain struggles there are no neutrals. Thus it has been with African Americans.

Uncle Tom (1922) outperforms all competition as pejorative slang for an African American who behaves in an obsequious fashion to curry favor with whites.

∷ ∷ ∷

And I've got to find out—whether we've been friends
all these years, or whether I've just been your favorite
Uncle Tom.
—James Baldwin: *Blues for Mister Charlie* (1964) 62

The bootlickers, **Uncle Toms**, lackeys, and stooges
of the white power structure have done their best to
denigrate Malcolm.
—Eldridge Cleaver: *Soul on Ice* (1968) 60

In the aren't-names-ironic department, Supreme Court Justice Clarence Thomas has come to personify the modern-day example of an African American who sides with the oppressors, largely because of his embrace of the hard right, damned-near-all-white wing of the Republican party and the fact that he has rejected whenever given the chance, any hint of affirmative action, the very program that made it possible for him to achieve what he has achieved. Thomas has denied repeatedly that he is an **Uncle Tom**, as in this article from *Jet Magazine* on November 14, 1994: —"Thomas was quoted as saying, 'I am not an **Uncle Tom**. I do not pay attention to that nonsense.'"

Uncle Tom (1937) also works as a verb, although tenses other than the present emerge a bit clumsily.

∷ ∷ ∷

We'd stand in line and wait for hours, smiling
and **Uncle Tomming** every time a doctor or nurse
passed by.
—Dick Gregory: *Nigger* (1964) 27

But for two bits, **Uncle Tom** a little—white cats
especially like that.
>   —Malcolm X: *Autobiography of Malcolm X* (1964) 47

Blue thundered, "You ugly, shit-colored **uncle-tomming**
motherfucker."
>   —Iceberg Slim: *Trick Baby* (1969) 230

   Uncle Tom—the noun—is seen both simplified as **Tom** (1959), embellished as **Doctor Tom** (1980), and feminized as **Aunt Thomasina**
(1963).

⁑ ⁑ ⁑

That's **Tom** making you nonviolent.
>   —Malcolm X: "Message to the Grass Roots"
>   (November 10, 1963), cited in Malachi
>   Andrews, *Black Talk* (1973) 68

It was on Madison Avenue and you had to be a real **Tom**.
>   —Claude Brown: *Manchild in the Promised Land*
>   (1965) 170

They sent in the middle-class black members of the
Human rights Commission, and the brothers laughed
at them and called them **Toms**.
>   —Tom Wolfe: *Radical Chic and Mau-Mauing*
>   *the Flak Catchers* (1970) 121

Doctor Thomas (1967) was first noted by Mario Pei in *The Story of the
English Language* (1967) and then collected from black teenagers in Philadelphia by Edith Folb in *Runnin' Down Some Lines* (1980). And then, the
rare femininization:

⁑ ⁑ ⁑

On the other side are New York activists led by Al
Sharpton and Alton Maddox Jr. They savage their

opponents, calling them "**Uncle Toms**" and "**Aunt Thomasinas**."
—*Bergen County Record* (April 25, 1990) B7

Uncle Tom—the verb—is also simplified as **Tom** (1963), which also is clumsy, at least as spelled, when straying from the present tense.

⠿ ⠿ ⠿

I '**Tomed**' for him and explained we were only listening to records.
—Babs Gonzales: *I Paid My Dues* (1967) 49

I lived in the ghetto. Yes, I **tommed**.
—William Nack: *My Turf* (2004) 167

Other personifications are the noun **Aunt Jemima** (1966), the verb **Jeff** (1960), and the noun **Stepin Fetchit** (1940). **Aunt Jemima**, of course, refers an iconic advertising image created by Quaker Oats, depicting a mammy-like, smiling, kerchiefed African-American woman of a certain weight. **Stepin Fetchit** is drawn from the obsequious stage persona of actor Lincoln Perry.

⠿ ⠿ ⠿

What I [Adam Clayton Powell] cannot abide are the black '**Aunt Jemimas**' who snuggle up to the white power structure for approbation by denouncing 'black power' and telling Mr. Charlie what he wants to hear."
—*San Francisco Examiner* (August 18, 1966)

"Naturally," the saleslady said, doing what Marsha Lee called "**jeffing**."
—Clarence Cooper: *The Scene* (1960) 34

The junkie bastard was **jeffing** on me.
—Iceberg Slim: *Pimp* (1969) 63

The one thing I knew is that I was not going to write one
of those disgraceful high-tech **Stepin Fetchit** things.
　　—Odie Hawkins: *Lost Angeles* (1994) 29

To this list, Clarence Barnhardt in his *Second Barnhardt Dictionary of New English* (1980) adds **Aunt Jane** (1963) and **Aunt Tabby** (1969).

Handkerchief head (1942) has the same fawning, submissive ring, harkening back to the rural south and Jim Crow days.

⁙ ⁙ ⁙

Especially as a photographer, an artist, not a corporate
handkerchief head.
　　—Alexis Pate: *Losing Absalom* (2005) 44

"Why not cut out all the old time "**handkerchief head**
waitresses" and recruit all young college "foxes."
　　—Babs Gonzales: *I Paid My Dues* (1967) 78

Malcolm X harkened back to slavery when he delineated modern-day African Americans as either field slaves or house slaves. **House nigger** (1970) remains a harsh epithet for those who curry favor.

⁙ ⁙ ⁙

HOUSE NIGGER—Uncle Tom is a HOUSE NIGGER.
　　—Malachi Andrews: *Black Talk* (1973) 78

In other words, you are a **house nigger**.
　　—Cleveland Barrett: *My Loaded AK-47 Volume 1*
　　　　(2007) 190

Boojie (1970), a corruption of bourgeois, is a contemptuous adjective applied to middle-class African Americans by working-class African Americans. It was collected by Edith Folb in Philadelphia in *Runnin' Down Some Lines* (1980) and is found throughout African-American literature.

⚡ ⚡ ⚡

"I pay you a thousand dollars a week and you can't
even get one **bougie** nigga!"
—Charles W. Moore: *A Brick for Mister Jones*
(2975) 62

Oreo (1968) is a relatively recent addition to the lexicon of disdain.
The allusion is excruciatingly simple—like the cookie, the person is
black on the outside, white on the inside.

⚡ ⚡ ⚡

She's a pure **Oreo**. You know, like the cookie, black
outside and white inside.
—Iceberg Slim: *The Naked Soul of Iceberg Slim*
(1971) 89

OREO—Someone Black on the outside and White on
the inside.
—Malachi Andrews: *Black Language* (1973) 97

In slang, there is no refuge for traitors to the race, just scorn, contempt, disdain, and derision. There are no two sides when it comes to
those who submissively ingratiate themselves with the dominant white
power structure.

Say What?

African-American slang is characterized by humor, creativity, and
double meaning. The vernacular permits communication with an independence not found in other types of expression.

In slave times, talking back was brutally suppressed. A slave spoke
openly under threat of harsh punishment. The slave Creole and then
African-American vernacular were rich with double meaning, which
allowed blacks to say one thing while meaning another. Even gestures
were subject to double meaning. Shane and Graham White wrote in

Stylin' (1998): "Even slaves who assumed the seemingly submissive down look could invest this gesture with ambiguous meanings."

Urban black vernacular English serves mutually reinforcing double functions. On the one hand, it leaves white America unable to communicate effectively in the black ghetto. Just as importantly, it renders the black speaker harmless, or at least seemingly harmless, to the dominant white power structure. Nobody put it more eloquently than Richard Pryor, who was quoted in the *New York Times Magazine* on April 27, 1975, as having said, "Niggers just have a way of telling you stuff and not telling you stuff."

Examples of double and hidden meanings may be found in "The World Upside Down" above. A black could say that someone was a **bad nigger** and the uninformed white man would think that this was derogatory, not the praise that it intends. Similarly, a black could say that a white man was a **square**, intended as a put-down, heard as praise.

Obfuscation of meaning is certainly a primary function of urban black vernacular. Four examples of dense jive speech from Dan Burley (1945), Lavada Durst (1953), and Babs Gonzales (1955) illustrate this point.

❊ ❊ ❊

> I dig that you're a solid Cat, and know each and every answer. And I'm hipped that you play the game, three ways sides and flats, and straight across the board. But, Jackson, you're flippin', and you ain't flappin'; you're floppin' and you ain't flyin' a-tall! Ole man, you're still wearing low quarters wile I'm stashing my stomps in a fine pair of nee-boots with laces long enough to tie up the Baer's Nephew, Joe, who really doesn't know.
> —Dan Burley: *Dan Burley's Original Handbook of Harlem Jive* (1945)

> On the late bright after you have put down your easy slave you drape yourself in shape and tam on the cuts where the cats are putting down much trash and everything is much solid. And our fly chick is looking most frantic and or short is all gassed up and ready to

roll because all the kitties know that rubber tires beats rubber heals.
—Lavada Durst: *The Jives of Dr. Hepcat* (1953)

About a deuce of black-and-whites ago, a stud from the natural lowlands arrived in the Apple. He copped him a hame as a delivery cat on Lenox Avenue. Everything was fine as wine until he cut into Hollywood eyes. My man Eddie, he dug her all the way. But after lamping her quit the scene daily the King of Shorts, he figured that he'd cool until his bread was long enough for him to sound her. One bright, about a deuce of ticks, he laid his story on a Harlem acquaintance named Congolene Freddy. He pulled Freddy's coat about his big eyes for this chick and how he'd pay any kind of dues to cop some long green. Freddy, being a post-graduate and a six-year New York man, knew the pig when he saw it. So, he yessed the boob for a few blacks and then laid down his spiel.
—Babs Gonzales: *A Manhattan Fable* (circa 1955)

And then there is the iconic "I speak jive" scene in the 1980 movie *Airplane*, a spoof of disaster movies. Two African-American passengers converse in jive:

❉ ❉ ❉

First jive dude: Shit man, that honky mus' be messin' my old lady. Got to be runnin' cold upside down his head, you know?
Second jive dude: Hey, home, I can dig it. You know he ain't gonna lay no mo' big rap up on you, man.
First jive dude: I say, hey sky, s'other s'ay I wan say?
Second jive dude: Uh!
First jive dude: Pray to J I get the same ol' same ol'.
Second jive dude: Eh! Yo knock yourself a pro slick gray matter live performas down take TCB'in man.

First jive dude: Hey, you know what they say. See a broad,
to get that booty yak 'em.
—*Airplane* (1980)

When the flight attendant, played by Lorna Patterson, admits that she cannot understand the passengers, a prim-looking white passenger, played by Barbara Billingsley, offers, "I speak jive" and proceeds to translate what the jive dudes are saying into standard English.

Double meaning and meaning hidden behind a mask of an impenetrable lexicon designed for sparing use but available for dense use allow African Americans freedom of speech not available in the standard register.

A Manner Rather Rude

At certain times and certain places, African-American slang is vulgar, hyperbolic, and full of bragging and boasting. To the extent that this is a linguistic reflection of an insurgent archetype, the hyperbole and vulgarity and bragging can be seen as elements of a resistance culture.

Attention must be paid not to overstate the case here.

Not all slang used by African Americans can be reasonably characterized as a gesture of resistance. Contemporary African-American slang, at least that large portion arising within hip-hop culture, is laced with commodity fetishism, materialism and material placebos, open and notorious misogyny, and glorification of substance abuse. Marxist theorists would—and do—characterize much of hip-hop culture as false consciousness or internalized oppression. Without engaging in an endless debate of limited interest and more limited authorial qualification, it can simply be acknowledged that not all manifestations of African-American culture fit the model of resistance behavior.

Similarly, not even all strong words and hyperbole in African-American slang can be reasonably characterized as gestures of resistance. Shock in and of itself is not revolutionary, although in their day Abbie Hoffman and Jerry Rubin may have disagreed. Sometimes, even in an oppressed people, vulgarity and hyperbole are just vulgarity and hyperbole for the sake of, yes, vulgarity and hyperbole.

Much has been written about the role of ritual insult and expressive role behavior in African-American culture. The dozens, selling tickets or woof tickets, signifying, jonesing, capping, snapping, and woofing are all types of verbal sparring that have been an African-American tradition. Ritual insult draws on coarse and vulgar language and is driven by equal parts of put-down and bragging, but it is difficult to see how it represents a manifestation of resistance. Ritual insult may, as many have argued, prepare young black men to accept insult without resorting to violence—a helpful survival skill in a world where insults from the oppressors are common and violent response to insult is dangerous, but not resistance. The coarse words and exaggeration and boasting of ritual insult represent linguistic horizontal violence and ego aggrandizement, but do not qualify as gestures of resistance.

Having dispensed with the exceptions—back to the rule. Not all vulgarity and hyperbole in African-American slang are expressions of resistance, but some is. When slang is an extension of an archetype of resistance, bragging, strong words, and embellishment rise to the status of resistance culture.

Bragging and boasting have always been characteristics of white American folk heroes, both real (Davy Crockett, Annie Oakley, Buffalo Bill Cody, Billy the Kid, Bonnie and Clyde, Pretty Boy Floyd, and Jesse James are a few) and fictional (Paul Bunyan, Casey Jones, Pecos Bill, Joe Magarac, and Gib Morgan). So too with African-American folk heroes—John Henry, Stagolee/Stackolee, Dolemite, and Shine. Eithne Quinn argues in *Nuthin' but a 'G' Thang* (2005) that the badman emerged in the twentieth century as an "emblem of poor black insurgency," and that the gangster in hip-hop culture is an "outlandish black archetype" and "a continuation of this vernacular tradition."

In this context, high-profile words such as **motherfucker, gangsta'**, and **pimp** can be seen as heroic expression and as rage against white oppression. Slang is not the main event in the main arena here, simply the supporting cast in the counter-narrative of the oppressed.

Although **motherfucker** is no longer the exclusive property of African Americans, its heritage is African American and its popularity is due to African-American usage. To hear **motherfucker**, listen to it as used by Redd Foxx, Richard Pryor, or Eddie Murphy. Yes, honorable mention to George Carlin, but the medals go to African Americans. Its struggle cred comes from the **bad motherfucker**, the tough, fearless archetype of resistance.

Motherfucker is a flexible word. In the first instance, it can be used to mean a truly despicable, loathsome person who is at least in theory capable of incest with his mother (1928). With slightly different tone, it can also mean simply a regular Joe, an average person (1958). The line between the two senses is membrane-thin. Malachi Andrews knew how thin that membrane is—"You can't express what it means. Anything before or after ain't what it is. Never has, never will be." *Black Language* (1973).

First—the despised person **motherfucker**, the figurative equivalent of one who would literally engage in the mother of all taboos, incest.

⚏ ⚏ ⚏

It's these respectable **motherfuckers** been doing all the dirt. They been stealing the colored folks blind, man.
—James Baldwin: *Another Country* (1962) 16

Dare any dirty **mother-fucker** in this place to come an stop me from stomping this bitch.
—Dick Gregory: *Nigger* (1962) 16

The cat in the corner said, "All you **motherfuckers** better keep still, because the next cat who moves is dead."
—Claude Brown: *Manchild in the Promised Land* (1965) 216

I said, "**Motherfucker**, don't be cussing at me."
—Bobby Seale: *Seize the time* (1970) 9

Fiddle with the tone and context dials and you have **motherfucker** as a neutral, or even positive term:

⚏ ⚏ ⚏

Originally, a derogatory term. Presently used as a term of either admiration or disgust, depending on the

moment and the emotional or intellectual point of view
when written or vocalized.
        —Robert deCoy: *The Nigger Bible* (1967) 33

The ubiquitous term **motherfucker**, once a serious
curse, is now an all-purpose word whose meaning is
entirely dependent on tone and context, as in "I love
that **motherfucker**."
        —Christina and Richard Milner: *Black Players*
        (1972) 46

You couldn't steal; you couldn't copycat a
motherfucker—or they put your ass in the back.
        —Bernie Mac: *Ain't Scared of You* (2001) 66

Motherfucker can also refer to a difficult thing or task (1958) and is
a common basis for comparison (1962).

⠶ ⠶ ⠶

Yo, your pop groovier-than-a-**motherfucker**.
        —Paul Beatty: *Tuff* (2000) 36

Damn, girl, it is hotter than a **motherfucker** up in here.
        —Dr. Dre: "Bar One" (2001)

If an all-purpose, rage-against-the-machine intensifier is needed, **motherfucking** (1897) will do the trick.

⠶ ⠶ ⠶

So this stud walk in and said: I want some
motherfucking meat. For my **motherfucking** cat. Not
too **motherfucking** lean. Not too **motherfucking** fat.
        —Roger Abrahams: *Deep Down in the Jungle*
        (1964) 199

You ain't nothin' but an old stupid God damn fool,
motherfucking asshole.
        —Bobby Seale: *A Lonely Rage* (1978) 24–25

Because **motherfucker** is so rude, there are a host of euphemisms, includ-ing **double-clutcher** (1967) and **double-clutching** (1964), **duck plucker** (1976), **emffeing** (1958), **furthermucker** (1965), **granny jazzer** (1977), **grungejumper** (1958), **mama-jammer** (1969), **mammy-fugger** (1998), **mammy-jammer** (1973), **mammyjamming** (1946), **mammy-screwing** (1963), **mammy-sucker** (1972), **momma-hopper** (1977), **motheren** or **mothering** (1959), **motherfather** (1992), **motherferyer** (1946), **motherflipping** (1961), **mother-for-you** (1957), **motherfugger** (1948), **motherfugging** (1948), **mothergrabbing** (1958), **motherhopper** (1977), **motherhugger**(1956), **motherhumper** (1963), **motherjumper** (1949), **motherjumping** (1950), **mother lover** (1950), **mother loving** (1951), **motherlumping** (1961), **mother-raper** (1959), **mother-raping** (1932), **mother-robbing** (1948), **motherscratcher** (2001), **motherseller** (1953), **motor scooter** (1960), **muddlefugging** (1961), and **poppa-lopper** (1977).

For the last fifteen years, the urban tough, the **gangsta**, has been the archetype of tough urban black youth. Granted, the **gangsta's** toughness is most often directed at other blacks, but his rage is the result of and ultimately directed at white oppression and when all is said and done he fits within the vernacular tradition of the archetype of resistance.

Gangster images are found in African-American slang before **gangsta** stormed onto the scene in the 1990s. David Claerbaut recorded **gangster** meaning marijuana in 1972, and there were the car-talk terms **gangster whitewalls** (1972), the **gangster lean** (1973) and **gangster doors, gang-ster fronts, gangster ride**, and **gangster walls** (1980).

※ ※ ※

Though you may not drive a great big Cadillac /
Gangster whitewalls, TV antennas in the back.
—Curtis Mayfield: "Just Be Thankful (For What
You've Got)" (1972)

Elijah had added some **gangster whitewalls** and now
he was on the scene, stylin' for the people who could
really dig such things.
—Odie Hawkins: *Chicago Hustle* (1977) 147

He put **gangster whitewall** tires on his ride and cruised through Cavalier Manor hawking drugs and supervising the guys working for him.

> —Nathan McCall: *Makes Me Wanna Holler* (1994) 124

Diamonds in the back, sunroof top / diggin' the scene with the **gangster lean**.

> —Massive Attack: "Be Thankful For What You've Got": (1991)

gangster doors Four-door sedan.
gangster fronts Style of dress associated with the gangster
gangster ride 1. Old-model car; 2. Any big car, especially one painted black
gangster stick Marijuana cigarette
gangster walls Wide white-walled tires

> —Edith Folb: *Runnin' Down Some Lines* (1980) 238–239

And then there was **gangsta** (1989). **Gangsta** stormed in with the rap group NWA:

⚌ ⚌ ⚌

"Gangsta, Gangsta!" That's what they're yellin
"It's not about a salary, it's all about reality"
"Gangsta, Gangsta! That's what they're yellin
"Hopin you sophisticated motherfuckers hear what I have to say"

> —NWA (Niggaz With Attitude): "Gangsta, Gangsta" (1989)

Interviewed in the *Los Angeles Times* (March 24, 1989) about the song and album "Straight Outta Compton," NWA member Ice Cube described the song as **gangsta rap** (1989). **Gangsta** was everywhere:

▓ ▓ ▓

The gangsta's back, the bank is fat / The **gangsta** mack,
in a gangsta 'llac.
   —Snoop Dogg: "Ten Lil' Crips"(2006)

Break out the champagne glasses and the motherfuckin
condoms / Have one on us aight? / Ain't nuttin but a
gangsta party.
   —2Pac: "2 of Amerikaz Most Wanted" (2004)

Cos it's the city / and for you to survive a nigga gotta be
a **gangsta**.
   —Dr. Dre: "A Nigga Witta Gun" (1992)

The **gangsta** was a continuation of the badman tradition in African-American popular culture. He was, more or less, a 1990s version of Stagolee and Dolemite, and the word **gangsta** and the new musical genre of **gangsta rap** were products of oppression no less than Stagolee and Dolemite. **Gangsta** was an expression of resistance in other respects. First, it was a horizontal assertion of west coast/Los Angeles-basin artistry in the face of domination of the rap field by East coast/New York artists. Of greater interest here, it was also a defiant movement opposing appropriation of the rap genre by the white entertainment establishment. Decades earlier, black jazz musicians had woven improvisation into the fabric of jazz, keeping black musical vernacular safe from white musicians who were imitating black styles. By striking such a defiant, hostile, and violent pose, **gangsta rap** defended the turf of rap by taunting white America—okay, appropriate this. Although **gangsta rap** has proved to be commercially lucrative, it has not lent itself to mainstream appropriation.

The final player (ha!) in the shocking/outlandish/hyperbolic derby of damn-the-man African-American slang is **pimp**. As a procurer of prostitutes, the word **pimp** dates back to 1607. In the black urban ghettos of the twentieth century, the world-upside-down viewpoint made outlaws heroes—numbers runners, confidence men, and **pimps** with their stables of prostitutes, all of whom were seen as smart enough to live well without working. The autobiographical fiction of Iceberg Slim and Donald Goines in the late 1960s and early 1970s propelled the procuring **pimp** to the pinnacle of counter-cultural icon status. With this status came any number of **pimp** compound nouns, including **pimp dust** (1980) for cocaine, **pimpmobile** (1972) for a showy luxury car, **pimp post** (1980) for an armrest for a car's driver's seat, **pimp roll** (1990) for a stylized walking style, **pimp shoes** (1972) for flashy shoes, **pimp stick** (1967) for a cigarette holder, **pimp sticks** (1972) for a wire coat hanger used to beat prostitutes, and **pimp suit** (1980) for a flashy suit.

As the prostitute-procuring **pimp** became a heroic expression of defiant culture, it is natural that the meaning of the word would evolve. In the early 1960s, **pimp** sprouted a second sense. Yes, a **pimp** still procured and/or lived off the earnings of a prostitute, but a **pimp** could also simply be an alluring, seductive man.

⠶ ⠶ ⠶

> **PIMP**: Originally a procurer, but because of the style of this profession, now used among this group to refer to any "smart" person.
> —Roger Abrahams: *Deep Down in the Jungle* (1964) 263

The next stop for **pimp** was life as an adjective meaning good, fashionable, excellent.

⠶ ⠶ ⠶

> "**Pimp**" as an adjective commonly means "sharp" or "beautiful."
> —Roger Abrahams: *Positively Black* (1970) 92

> Sometimes a group of buddies who ran together were "stone **pimp**," as the phrase went, would move straight into the poverty program.
> —Tom Wolfe: *Radical Chic & Mau-Mauing the Flak Catchers* (1970) 132

At roughly the same time, **pimping** came to apply to a stylized style of walking, thus focusing on the outward and physical manifestations of the man's style, not the source of his income.

⁂ ⁂ ⁂

PIMPING: A fine steppin' walk. Dig one way you can. Relax. Completely. Stick your head ahead or behind you. Put your butt back and let your arms hang. Now as you walk, bounce form heel to toe; let your head float with the rhythm of the body; swing your body left, right, left, right; throw your chest out a bit and bring it back, and do it again. Think cool, dress cool, and don't forget, be cool.
—Malachi Andrews: *Black Language* (1973) 67

By the 1990s, **pimp** as a fashionably flashy, alluring man came to dominate rap lyrics and in this sense was found in Clarence Major's up-dated dictionary of African-American slang (*Juba to Jive,* 1994), Robert Chapman's slang dictionary (*Dictionary of American Slang,* Third Edition, 1994), and college lexicons collected by Pamela Munro (*UCLA Slang 3,* 1997), Connie Eble (*University of North Carolina Campus Slang,* Spring 1997), and Judi Sanders (*Da Bomb,* 1997).

Then came **pimp** as a new verb. To **pimp** (1972) originally meant to procure or live off the earnings of a prostitute or prostitutes.

⁂ ⁂ ⁂

You sure **pimped** up a storm when I was a kid. What happened? Why are you steering for this crap joint?
—Iceberg Slim: *Pimp* (1969) 94

Just because I don't want to **pimp** Amelia or anybody else?
—Bobby Seale: *A Lonely Rage* (1978) 153

To **pimp** (1993) now became to render flashy or showy, to accessorize.

※ ※ ※

You wish you had my fly ass girlfriend, and my **pimped**
out ride.
—David Leonard: *Screens Fade to Black* (2006) 149

In 2004, MTV debuted the soon-to-be-very-popular "Pimp My Ride"
series, an irrefutable sign that the new **pimp** verb had made the scene.

The supreme moment for the new **pimp** came in 2005 when the
Ninth District Court of Appeal, the honorable Carlos Bea dissenting, af-
firmed the decision of a United States District Court for Montana Judge
Donald Molloy that Evil Knievel's claim that ESPN had defamed him
through a caption on an extreme sports website identifying Knievel as a
pimp was not actionable because **pimp's** first meaning as a procurer of
prostitutes no longer held up. **Pimp** was praise, not disrespect, and time
had passed Knievel by. Alluring but not procuring—how outlandish!

Ebonics

It would be wrong to discuss African-American vernacular without a
mention of Ebonics, a theory about black language that incurred the ire
and wrath and conservatives in the late 1990s. The term "Ebonics" was
coined in 1973 to describe the study of the linguistic and paralinguistic
features of the language of black people, especially its cultural unique-
ness, its African roots, and its independence from standard English.

Ebonics was a theory and a term that was barely known outside the
academic community until December 1996 when the Oakland (California) Unified School District Board of Education passed a resolution of-
ficially recognizing "the existence, and the cultural and historic bases of
West and Niger-Congo African Language Systems, and each language as
the predominantly primary language of African-American students" and
resolving to "devise and implement the best possible academic program
for imparting instruction to African-American students in their primary
language."

The controversy that arose when the resolution was publicized in
January 1997 was intense, fierce, and even vicious. Most of the criticism, and certainly the loudest criticism of the Board's resolution displayed a nearly complete ignorance as to what the Board had actually

resolved, and was based in large part on an incorrect conflation of dialect with slang and then a further conflation of slang with profanity, leading the critics to believe that the school board was advocating teaching profanity.

The theory survived the withering criticism of 1997, but the term remained one generally avoided by linguists who prefer "African-American Vernacular English" or "African-American Non-standard English." In any event, the language of resistance of African Americans has had its admirers and supporters.

CHAPTER 3

Prisoners

Short of slavery, incarceration is the ultimate oppression. Prison authorities have nearly complete control over a prisoner's time and movement. Boredom and brutality are fixtures of prison life. Most prisoners have experienced oppression in the free world, and they bring this experience with them. Most prisoners have tendencies toward violence that place them well out of the X-axis compared to the norms and mores of the free world. Horizontal violence abounds in prison, in the form of prison gangs with inter-racial and intra-racial overtones, purely racial cliques, and one-on-one dislikes and vendettas. As is the case in many same-sex institutions (the U.S. Navy adage that "if you're underway, it isn't gay" needs no explanation), situational homosexual behavior is a fact of life in prison, and in some instances it is as much a representation of violent behavior as it is of sexual behavior. In his 1950 *Dictionary of American Underworld Lingo*, Hyman Goldin described prisons as "the professional finishing schools of the underworld." Today, they have lost the glamour of professional, specialized criminals and are little more than the finishing schools of oppression.

In short, prison is a separate reality from the free world. In prison, there are few fine lines of oppression. The domination and subjugation, whether cruel or benign, is clear and unambiguous. Captivity, confinement, and the utter control that prison authorities exercise over the life of prisoners all shape to a powerful degree the language of prisoners, many of whom bring with them slang forged by oppression. Prison life is the result of a collision of races, cultures, generations, and hometowns, bound by the common denominator of a felony conviction. A common transactional slang is an inevitable result of both the oppression of prison life and the disparate backgrounds of prisoners. While the observation by Gilbert Encinas in *Prison Argot* (2001) that "The language of the largest ethnic group tends to dominate the prison lingo" may be true, pieces of slang from smaller groups are mixed with the dominant slang to create a new beast, an amalgamated prison argot.

Some argue that prisoner vernacular is in large part code designed and used to hide the meaning of prisoner conversation from guards. The fact is that guards pick up the meaning of prisoner vernacular quite quickly, even if they sound awkward and off-balance when using it themselves. Moreover, in prison only certain words need to be secret. The number of these keep-a-secret words is quite low, and for this reason the code theory fails to explain the largest part of prison slang.

No—prison slang is primarily used as a gesture of resistance in a setting where open deviance in the form of escape, riot, or isolated attacks on guards is quickly and convincingly crushed. As it does with oppressed elsewhere, prison slang serves to establish a positive, proud identity for prisoners, while disparaging and mocking prison authorities and prisoners who side with prison authorities against fellow prisoners. The prisoner's greatest enemy—time—is an important subject within the prison vernacular lingo. Finally, prison slang is used to describe open acts of uprising, such as escape.

Prisoners are all too conscious of the unique nature of their language and they exhibit their pride by showing the language off, calling attention to it, marketing it. Prisoners have a long and established history of producing their own slang dictionaries. The crown jewel of prison and crime dictionaries is the *Dictionary of American Underworld Lingo* edited by Hyman E. Goldin (1950), which boasts of a Board of Underworld Advisors and which proclaims that it was written "in the only way possible, by men who have served a long apprenticeship 'on the turf,' and followed additional courses in the nation's prisons, the professional finishing schools of the underworld." The tradition continued with *Prison Slang* (1992) by William Bentley (five years, burglary, Arizona State Prison) and James Corbett (five years, armed robbery, Indiana State Prison and five years, armed robbery, Arizona State Prison) and with Gary Farlow's *Prison-ese* (2002). All of the terms included by Farlow were collected over a period of ten years while incarcerated in the North Carolina Department of Corrections, Division of Prisons.

Honor Among Thieves

To society, to prison authorities, and even to the families of some prisoners, a prisoner has fallen as low as a person can fall. The brutality and dehumanization of prison life can easily crush a person's identity and self-esteem. As an antidote, prisoners find identity and pride through bodybuilding, tattoos, prison gangs, through fundamentalist religion or radical political ideology, and through a vernacular that finds worth where others have not found worth.

The first linguistic step in restoring honor to prisoners is to identify prison as something other than prison. The most common slang terms for prison are **big house** (1913), **joint** (1933), **pen** (1884) as an abbreviated "penitentiary," and **stir** (1851).

❖ ❖ ❖

"Strebhouse and Stevens spent a stretch in the **big house**," I said.
—Mickey Spillane: *I, the Jury* (1947) 111

In fact, their fate was often worse. Suicide. Dope addiction and the d.t.'s. The **big house** and the nuthouse.
—Jim Thompson: *The Grifters* (1963) 24

Zeke gave me a quick matchbook education on how to live and exist in the **big house**.
—Sonny Barger: *Hell's Angel* (2000) 197

You can be charged in State on one and Federal on the other so that when you walk out of the State **joint** the Federals meet you at the door.
—William Burroughs: *Junkie* (1953) 95

I was arrested in Arizona, the **joint** absolutely the worst **joint** I've ever been in.
> —Jack Kerouac: *On the Road* (1957) 231

In the **Joint** I always get in top shape; no coke, no pot, no pussy, so you work out.
> —Edwin Torres: *Carlito's Way* (1975) 41

"First I want revenge because their fathers sent my old man to die in the **pen**." The Crawler's eyes were blazing with hate as he spoke.
> —Chester Gould: *Dick Tracy Meets the Night Crawler* (1945) 40

Yeah, they're from Newark and they done time in the state **pen**.
> —Piri Thomas: *Down These Mean Streets* (1967) 213

I'm sorry man, I shoulda picked you up personally at the **pen**.
> —*Reservoir Dogs* (1992)

I've been in the **stir** and I've had my miseries, but all in all life's been good to me.
> —Mezz Mezzrow: *Really the Blues* (1946) 3

Few men, once they get outside, keep to the arrangements they make in **stir**.
> —Charles Raven: *Underworld Nights* (1956) 31

Shit, I may as well be in **stir**.
> —Elmore Leonard: *Killshot* (1989) 165

Humorous ameliorations of prison are common, most commonly **cross-bar hotel** (1865), **graybar hotel** (1970), or simply **hotel** (1845).

⠶ ⠶ ⠶

"You boys are going to the **cross-bar hotel**," Travis said.
—Finis Farr: *Black Champion* (1969) 20

Anyone who has spent serious time in the **gray-bar hotel** chain is left with certain kinds of signatures on his person.
—James Lee Burke: *Swan Peak* (2008) 115

Hotel: Detention cell house.
—John Armore: *Dictionary of Desperation* (1976) 34

Other terms referencing institutional life other than behind bars were collected by Vincent Monteleone in 1949 (**graystone college**, **county hotel** for a local jail), John Armore in 1976 (**Waldorf-Astoria**), James Harris in 1989 (**academy**, **college**), and William Bentley in 1992 (**Disneyland** for a prison with lax rules, **school of crime**). Monteleone collected the humorous **alma mater** as a prison in which a convict has served time, while Armore recorded **the flats** as referring to the ground floor in a tiered prison. In a published-from-prison 1991 pamphlet *30 and a Wake-Up*, L.V. McNelis added **camp** to the list of metaphorical, institutional allusions used in prison slang to describe prison. In a quaintly sexist vein, Monteleone included **chicken coop** and **hen house** as terms used by male prisoners to describe a women's prison.

Gladiator school (1981) is a common, grimly humorous slang term that prisoners use to describe a violent prison.

⠶ ⠶ ⠶

Not that it matters. Joints are all the same, **gladiator schools**.
—Seth Morgan: *Homeboy* (1990) 161

He'd been sent to Coxsackie Correctional Facility, a maximum-security prison that houses mostly felons in

their late teens and early twenties, known by correction officers as "**gladiator school**."
—Jennifer Wynn: *Inside Rikers* (2001) 28

Hammer was also someone I knew from **Gladiator School**.
—K.C. Carceral: *Prison, Inc.* (2006) 50

While the humor with respect to **gladiator school** is dark, the other comparisons to hotels, camps, and learning institutions are all kinder and gentler than "prison." The walls and bars do not disappear, but the vocabulary used to describe prison blunts the sharp reality.

Just as prisoners use slang to tart up prison, they either obscure or domesticate their cells. The dim reality of bleak is cloaked by **kip**, originally (1859) used to mean a bed but recorded by Goldin in 1950 to mean a cell, and by **drum** (1909).

⠶ ⠶ ⠶

He's in the big house for all day and night, a new fish jammed into a **drum** with a cribman, who acts like a gazoonie.
—*San Francisco Examiner* (August 17, 1976) 26

Drum A prison cell.
—William Bentley: *Prison Slang* (1992) 6

Domesticity is established by **apartment** (Monteleone, 1949), **hut** and **den** (Goldin, 1950), **house** (Bentley, 1992), and **cabin** (Hilderbrant, 1998), referring to a cell with a sheet draped over the bars to create a private space.

What, then, of prisoners? There is no affirmation or self-esteem in "prisoner," and so in steps prison vernacular to rename. Before disposing with the old, there is a fascinating embrace of standard English. The standard **inmate** takes on, in the language of prisoners, a negative tone.

※ ※ ※

Inmate New prisoner, new breed, usually selfish, unproven.
　　　　—James Harris in Morris Camhi: *The Prison Experience* (1989) 33

Conversely and still within striking distance of standard English, a **solid convict** (1979) is a tough, reliable prisoner.

※ ※ ※

I guess he's a man in most respects, a **solid convict** from all I hear about him, but also a sissy, queen, or whatever you wanta call 'em.
　　　　—Norman Mailer: *The Executioner's Song* (1979) 516

Moreover, he was a **solid convict** and Jimmy Barry was a reputed stool pigeon.
　　　　—Edward Bunker: *Education of a Felon* (2000) 134

If economy in word-count is vital, the simple **convict** (1989) can be used in a vernacular sense to refer to a trustworthy, experienced prisoner.

※ ※ ※

Convict Stand up guy, older timer, someone who understands and believes in the code of ethics, hard core supporter of those ethics.
　　　　—James Harris in Morris Camhi: *The Prisoner Experience* (1989) 30

"Man, I can't stand all these inmates. I'm from the old school when it was just us **convicts**."
　　　　—Gary Farlow: *Prison-ese* (2002) 15

Courage, trustworthiness, and an adherence to a prison code of ethics are characteristics that underlie the prison slang lexicon applied to fellow prisoners. Monteleone (1949) recorded **fraternity brother**. Amore (1976) added **citizen, highlighter** (a spokesman for a group of prisoners), **known man, rock,** and **thorough** as a noun. Cardozo-Freeman (1984) contributed **back-me-up, heavy, people,** and **senior citizen**. James Harris (1989) logged **brother** and **bro, ace-deuce, co-signer, good wood, road dog,** and **shot-caller** as laudatory descriptors of a fellow prisoner. Encinas (2001) noted **yard dog** and **dog,** while Farlow (2002) added **rap dog**.

Special attention is paid to one type of prisoner, someone with a passion and at least a perceived expertise in exploring legal arguments to challenge convictions and prison conditions. The most common term is **jailhouse lawyer** (1926), which connotes some degree of admiration.

❘❘ ❘❘ ❘❘

They pound out their pleas on a battered typewriter, or a "**jailhouse lawyer**" does it for them. There's such a man in almost every prison.
— Harold Coy: *The First Book of the Supreme Court* (1958) 10

Homer had played **jailhouse lawyer** and promised a cellmate he could spring him for fifty dollars.
— Walter Wagner: *The Golden Fleecers* (1966) 24

Manson was enough of a **jailhouse lawyer** to know that I couldn't use anything he told me unless I'd first informed him of his constitutional rights.
— Vincent Bugliosi: *Helter Skelter* (1974) 306

To **jailhouse lawyer** Monteleone (1949) added **writ bug** and Bentley (1992) added **yardbird lawyer**.

In an institution where a person's movement is nearly completely controlled, there is some irony in the use of **car** to mean a group of prisoners who rely on each other for friendship and support. James Harris (1989) first recorded the term, as well as **passenger** for someone who is a member of a **car**. Lexicographical pioneer Reinhold Aman recorded **car** in his 1996 *Hillary Clinton's Pen Pal*, as well as **in the car** and **out of the car** to describe a prisoner's relationship with a **car**.

Adjectives are the final step in the identity-affirmation aspect of prisoner slang. **Con-wise** (1912), **joint-wise** (1935), and **jail-wise** (1967) are all used to mean experienced and sophisticated in the ways and mores of incarceration.

⁑ ⁑ ⁑

We call it being **con-wise**. They, just like us convicts, adopt this slang and use it in the normal habitat of working here.
　　—Bruce Jackson: *Outside the Law* (1972) 51

And he had, indeed, become **con-wise**, gleaning whatever bits of information he needed from the men who shared his cell blocks.
　　—Ann Rule: *The Stranger Beside Me* (2000) 18

The perps might be **con-wise** and they may have the cunning of animals, but when it comes to successfully confronting the system, they're charging uphill.
　　—James Lee Burke: *The Tin Roof Blowdown* (2007) 29

Released **joint-wise** dealers decided to devote their expertise to the pill market.
　　—Chicano Pinto Research Project: *The Los Angeles Pinto* (1974) 56

When I returned to my housing unit I discussed this with some of the older **joint-wise** cons who I worked with.
　　—Wayne Wooden: *Men Behind Bars* (1984) 211

Now the reason for this is I'm **jail wise**. I know how to
get over. I know what I'm supposed to do.
> —Andrews Vachss: *The Life-Style Violent Juvenile*
> (1979) 251

I wasn't what you would call **jail-wise** or nothing like
that but I knew how to take care of myself.
> —Darrell Steffensmeier: *The Fence* (1986) 39

"This boy was **jail-wise** already," Murray reminded the
jurors.
> —Michael Newton: *Stolen Away* (2000) 314

To this list of standards, Ross (2002) adds **schooled** as a term of praise
meaning well-versed in prison life.

The slang of prisoners is also used to name the fellow convicted
felon with whom you happen to be sharing a small cell. Just as a room-
mate becomes a roomie, a cellmate becomes, simply enough, a **cellie**
(1966).

❊ ❊ ❊

"It goes like this, **cellie**," he says. "The cop comes by
here three times a day, right?"
> —David Harris: *I Shoulda Been Home Yesterday*
> (1976) 30

I'd rather have a **cellie**. Someone to talk to. My **cellie**
was with me at another prison. Here you have a choice
and can get a cell partner.
> —Gary Melton: *The Law as a Behavioral*
> *Instrument* (1986) 228

Older but less common is **bunkie** or **bunky** (1858), and from the brave
new world of modular cells comes **cubie** (1991).

Screw the Screw

As is the case with the lexicon of most oppressed groups, the slang of prisoners demonstrates a complete scorn and disrespect for their oppressors—the men and women of the criminal justice system.

Prison guards have the greatest contact with and control over the lives of prisoners. While prison slang is resplendent with terms for guards, three terms dominate the field—**screw** (1812), **bull** (1893), and **hack** (1914).

⁞⁞ ⁞⁞ ⁞⁞

We clambered out and stood in line to have our handcuffs removed. Two "**screws**" started at each end of the line unlocking the cuffs.
—Iceberg Slim: *Pimp* (1969) 49

Line **screw**: A correctional officer who works in the cell block.
—John Armore: *Dictionary of Desperation* (1976) 39

The average **screw** has the job because he isn't smart enough to wash automobiles.
—Jake La Motta: *Raging Bull* (1997) 201

High on the north block wall he glimpsed a gun **bull**.
—Malcolm Braly: *On the Yard* (1967) 4

For the convict, he has other names, such as "screw" "**bull**" "hack" and many others which are mostly uncomplimentary.
—Lou Torok: *Straight talk fro Prison* (1974) 114

He killed a **hack**, and they had to send him to Materwann.
—Claude Brown: *Manchild in the Promised Land* (1965) 370

He wouldn't have hurt the kids, but the **hack** would
have had an accident one day in prison.
>—Vincent Charles Teresa: *My Life in the Mafia*
>(1973) 302

The new night **hack** was much tighter.
>—Peter Brock: *These Strange Criminals* (2004) 468

Prisoners have dozens of other terms for guards. Of special derisive
interest are those that build on the pig metaphor. Armore (1976) recorded **swine**, and Cardoso-Freeman (1984) recorded **hog pen** and **pig
station** as the control room where guards work. Sadistic guards who dis-
turb the delicate system of compromise which prisoners establish with
their guards have special names. Goldin (1950) recorded **ball-breaker**;
Cardoso-Freeman (1984) added **dick-smacker**.

Prison authorities consider guards who are used to quell disturbances
or extract recalcitrant prisoners to and from their cells to be elite defend-
ers of order. Prisoners see them differently, dismissing them as the **goon
squad** (1967) or **boom squad** (2000).

⁙ ⁙ ⁙

In less than a minute the door flew open and three
guards entered on the double. "The **goon squad**," Nunn
whispered to Manning.
>—Malcolm Braly: *On the Yard* (1967) 34

Goon squad is a term used to denote a group of officers
who beat inmates for breaking prison rules.
>—Dae Chang: *The Prison* (1972) 327

They had their **goon squad**, an assault force who would
rush in with tear gas and weapons.
>—Lori Andrews: *Black Power, White Blood* (1999) 127

Depending on who you ask, the ESU, or "**boom
squad**," is a group of dedicated officers with the

toughest job on the island or a bunch of testosterone-
fueled thugs who get a rush from brawling with the
inmates.
        —*Village Voice* (December 19, 2000)

When it comes to a prison warden, prison slang veers between the
chumminess of ameliorative comparisons to other institutions and the
scorn found in terms for guards. Monteleone (1949) recorded **big head,
deacon, dean of men, father time, king screw, main screw**, and **old
man**. Goldin (1950) added **braid** and **skipper**.

Rats and Snitches

In a society that is as closed and oppressive as prison, the line between them and us is a bright and clear line, and there is little-to-zero
tolerance for prisoners who align themselves with prison authorities.
The venerable free-world terms **snitch** (1785) and **rat** (1902) for informer are used. In the **rat** vein, Bentley (1992) recorded **cheese-eater**
(1886), which also enjoys free-world usage. Building on **snitch** is **snitch
kite** (1967):

⠵⠵ ⠵⠵ ⠵⠵

You've never written a **snitch-kite**, have you?
        —Frank Elli: *The Riot* (1967) 86

Admin was receiving far more **snitch kites** (notes sent
up front to staff when an inmate wants to inform on
others).
        —Bill Valentine: *Gangs and their Tattoos* (2000) 12

Those who fall short of absolute treason include Ersine's **stockholder**
(1933) for a prisoner who curries favor from the authorities, Goldin's
state man (1950) for a trustee, and Armore's **ad man** (1976) for a prisoner whose interests appear to be aligned with those of the prison ad-
ministration. Those who curry favor are said to **handshake** (1933) or
hang on the leg (1992). The prisoner who fraternizes with guards is dis-
missed as a **walkie-talkie** (Bentley, 1992) while he who fails to exercise

discretion while talking with fellow prisoners in the vicinity of guards is a **radio** (Harris, 1976).

There is a specialized prison slang vocabulary for dealing with traitors. The lucky ones are simply beaten or **tuned up** (Harris, 1989), or given a **blanket party** (1976)—those dishing out the punishment throw a blanket over the offender and severely beat him with the safety of anonymity.

❇ ❇ ❇

> **Blanket party** Severe beating (usually given to an informer) by more than one individual.
> —John Armore: *Dictionary of Desperation* (1976) 20

> I could easily end up the subject of a **blanket party** while I was sleeping.
> —Mark Lynch: *Walk with Me* (2006) 66

Other drastic sanctions include being thrown from an upper tier and thus getting a **flying lesson** (Bentley, 1992) or being burned in your cell, a **burn-out** (Glover, 1974) or **barbecue** (Bentley, 1992).

AT-TI-CA!

Overt acts of resistance in prison are rare, but are deeply etched in our collective memory. We remember vividly the futility and brutality of the Attica uprising/riot in September 1971, the real-life escape of John Dillinger in 1933, the fictional escape of Morgan Freeman in *The Shawshank Redemption,* and the real-life (Frank Morn and the Anglin brothers) slash fictional (Clint Eastwood) escapes from Alcatraz in 1962. Prisoners have a specialized vocabulary for these rare, desperate acts of open resistance.

Prisoners are often expected to work, and so refusing to work emerges as a logical act of resistance. Goldin (1950) recorded **buck** as a verb meaning to refuse a work assignment in prison, and Jackson (1972) recorded it as a noun meaning a sit-down strike in prison. Still in the non-violent school of resistance, Armore (1976) collected **stay-out** as a concerted refusal by prisoners to return to their cells.

Many prisoners are in prison because of violent crimes, and it is not surprising that their resistance is at times violent. The prison riot is the epitome of violent resistance, and is referred to as a **kick-over** (1950).

⁜ ⁜ ⁜

"I heard some screw got his lemon kicked in in that mess-hall **kick-over**."
> —Hyman Goldin: *Dictionary of Underworld Lingo* (1950) 116

During a riot, **airmail** (Bentley, 1992) refers to objects thrown by prisoners in upper tiers down upon prisoners and guards below. From the confines of the cell, a prisoner can throw feces—**brown trout** (Bentley, 1992) at guards outside the cell.

Escape is perhaps the quintessence of overt prisoner resistance, yet "escape" is unknown as a noun; the act is either obscured or humorously ameliorated. Wentworth and Flexner (*Dictionary of American Slang*, 1948) recorded **breeze**, Montelene (1949) left us **bush parole** and **leg bail**, and Goldin (1950) collected **cornfield clemo** and **mope**. Building on the nouns, Goldin gave **cop a breeze** and **cop a mope** as verbal phrases.

> Harold Wentworth and Stuart Flexner: *Dictionary of American Slang* (1948) 62
> Vincent Monteleone: *Criminal Slang* (1949) 39, 144
> Hyman Goldin: *Dictionary of Underworld Lingo* (1950) 50, 141, 49

Rabbit metaphors abound in the lexicon of prison escape. **Rabbit blood** (Goldin, 1950) and **rabbit fever** (Ragen, 1962) describe an obsessive urge to escape. The metaphor goes further:

⁜ ⁜ ⁜

He said, "In spite of the **rabbit** in this man I want him transferred to Ramsey construction immediately."
> —Bruce Jackson: *In the Life* (1972) 322

Spring was known as **rabbit season**, and four men ran
off during the first week of good weather.
    —Malcolm Braly: *On the Yard* (1967) 323

Rabbit foot (N) An escaped prisoner.
    —Vincent Monteleone: *Criminal Slang* (1949) 188

Deviating from the bunny image, **scram heat** (Ragen, 1962) is another
term used for the strong urge to attempt an escape. Returning to the
animal kingdom, **dog bait** (1972) is a prisoner abandoned by other prisoners during a group escape in the hope that the prison tracking dogs
will focus on his scent.

❈ ❈ ❈

Everybody in escaping down here, they're looking
for what we call **dog bait**. Unless you're with a guy
personally, you're going to try to feed them to the dogs
so you can get away.
    —Bruce Jackson: *In the Life* (1972) 217

    A dozen words, more or less, are used with some regularity meaning
"to escape." Monteleone (1949) recorded **fly the coop, go over the wall,
go over the hill,** and **bust the jug. Go over the hill** (1912) is older, and a
strong variant that like **go over the wall** is used in the military meaning
to desert.

❈ ❈ ❈

The other half dozen sick cons nearby knew we were
going over the hill.
    —Red Rudensky: *The Gonif* (1970) 14

Goldin (1950) added **blow stir, crack out, hit the hump,** and **spread
the eagle**.

Variations on "crash" are popular in slang escape verbs—**crash-out** (1940) as an escape, **crash out** (1949), and the abbreviated **crash** (1970) verbs.

:: :: ::

He's on the lam from a pen back east, **crashed out** with twenty years to serve of a thirty-year bank-robber rap.
— Jim Thompson: *A Swell-Looking Babe* (1954) 77

Spring (1904) is another frequently used slang verb of escape.

:: :: ::

By this time Bow and Emil Burbacher were **sprung** from The School and showed up on the Corner again.
—Mezz Mezzrow: *Really the Blues* (1946) 20

What are you talking about, Rollie? We're **springing** 'em?
—*Gone in 60 Seconds* (2000)

T...............i..............m.............e.................

Time is the single most critical issue in prison life. Abstract, philosophical questions about time—what it is, whether the future and past are real, whether the past and future are infinite—are not the issue. The issue is the central fact that prison confines a prisoner's time and space. Time, not prison authorities or rival political gangs, is a prisoner's nemesis.

One cannot resist time, but one can create a vocabulary to confine time, at least linguistically. In the nineteenth century, British slang abounded with nautical terms, a reflection of British naval supremacy. So too does prison slang abound with time-related terms, a reflection of the central role played by time and the need to affect with words that which cannot be affected with acts.

The word "time" figures in several prison slang terms and expression. To **do your time** (1962) is to serve your prison sentence with some degree of dignity and control. To **do your own time** (1954) is to mind your own business while serving your sentence. The ultimate prison wisdom is to **do your time, don't let your time do you** (1973).

⚎ ⚎ ⚎

> **Do your time** a day at a time, and **do your own time**
> and no one else's.
> > —Central Committee for Conscientious
> > Objectors: *Handbook for Conscientious Objectors*
> > (1954) 64

> Only by the strict adherence to each and every one can
> you **do your time**.
> > —Joseph Ragen: *Inside the World's Toughest Prison*
> > (1962) 61

> He **did the time**; he didn't **let the time do him**.
> > —Donald Goines: *White Man's Justice* (1973) 201

> Peter was advised by one jailhouse lawyer to "**do your
> time, don't let your time do you**."
> > —Donald Connery: *Guilty Until Proven Innocent*
> > (1977) 107

> Surviving prison without self-inflicted scars was
> mentioned as a sign of being able to **do your time**.
> > —Alison Liebling: *Suicides in Prison* (1992) 166

> One thing he had learned early, you **do your own time**
> in prison. You don't do anyone else's time for them.
> Keep your head down. **Do your own time**.
> > —Neil Gaiman: *American Gods* (2001) 6

Still on the time derivatives, **hard time** (1927), a prison sentence that because of the objective conditions of the prison and/or the subjective condition of the prisoner is especially difficult or debilitating.

⠿ ⠿ ⠿

Manning did **hard time** and the time was hard on him.
—Malcolm Braly: *On the Yard* (1967) 172

People wouldn't let me write for a while, I had to get a
clearance, and this took a long time. So I did **hard time**
because of this.
—David Petersen: *Criminal Life* (1972) 172

"Served his felony sentence in Raiford. They got a
prison there, Coop, makes Attica look like a beauty
school. Bailor did **hard time**. Real **hard time**."
—Linda Fairstein: *Cold Hit* (1999) 331

So I did **hard time** because of this. I couldn't come in
off the streets, is the thing.
—David Ward: *Women's Prison* (2007) 160

Monteleone (1949) recorded the variant **tough time**. Prewitt and
Schaeffer (1962) collected **clock** as referring to a prisoner at the start of
his sentence, while Farlow (2002) added **time-stretcher** as an annoying
fellow prisoner whose very presence seems to make time pass slowly.

The term "sentence" is a legal term, used by the oppressor, not by the
oppressed. **Rap** (1927) or **bit** (1866) are the two terms most commonly
used by prisoners to mean a sentence.

⠿ ⠿ ⠿

They mentally calculated Murray's age, and they
figured this for a prison **rap**.
—Evan Hunter: *The Blackboard Jungle* (1954) 79

He got sent to Starke on a homicide, shot some dude
he was supposed to be bringing in. Doing his **rap**, he
was the man up there among the Latinos.
—Elmore Leonard: *Riding the Rap* (1995) 29

He was sent up for his first real **bit** when he was 16.
—Hubert Selby Jr.

By the time he was twenty-three he had done four **bits**
in the joint.
—Iceberg Slim: *Pimp* (1969) 33

By this time his looks had coarsened some as a result of
his **bit** in San Quentin at the end of the '50s.
—Herbert Huncke: *Guilty of Everything* (1990) 95

Just as the noun "sentence" is avoided, the verbal phrase "serve a sentence" is rarely heard. Most commonly, a prisoner will speak of **jailing** (1967) with a certain proud and positive spin.

※ ※ ※

But you like **jailing**, Red. Nunn didn't.
—Malcolm Braly: *On the Yard* (1967) 325

Then he stepped out on the gallery, slamming the door
behind him with the experience of a convict who has
been **jailing** for a long time.
—Donald Goines: *Black Gangster* (1977) 8

I told him, he wouldn't listen. He never learned how to
jail. You know, live in a place like that.
—Elmore Leonard: *Stick* (1983) 173

Jailin' was an art form and lifestyle both. The style
was walkin' slow, drinkin' plenty of water, and doin'
your own time; the art was lightin' cigarettes from wall
sockets, playin' the dozens, cuttin' up dream jackpots,
and slowin' your metabolism.
—Seth Morgan: *Homeboy* (1990) 122

As a prisoner nears the end of his sentence—no, make that his **rap** or **bit**—he is said to be **short** (1967).

⁝⁝ ⁝⁝ ⁝⁝

> I'm so **short** now I can taste the street, and it's like I can't believe I'm here and the rules and regulations just aren't meant for me any more.
> —Piri Thomas: *Down These Mean Streets* (1967) 303

> "Well," I said, "you're a lot **short**er now than you were from the jump."
> —A. S. Jackson: *Gentleman Pimp* (1973) 130

This is an abbreviated form of **short-timer** (Dill, *Current Slang*, Winter 1966).

The final day of sentence is known as a **wake-up** (Goldin, 1950), suggesting that the prisoner simply wakes up and is released.

⁝⁝ ⁝⁝ ⁝⁝

> "Shit!" John exclaimed, "you ain't got nothing but a **wake-up**. You can do that shit on top of your head, man."
> —Donald Goines: *White Man's Justice, Black Man's Grief* (1973) 192

Similarly, any portion of a sentence served while on parole is a **tail**. (Bentley, 1992).

When it comes to the terminology used to describe prison sentences, prisoners often borrow slang from the free world used to describe currency or bets. More than serving simply as carry-over from the underworld life outside prison walls, the use of gambling slang blunts—and defies—the grim reality of time passed while incarcerated.

A one-year sentence: **one-spot** (Monteleone, 949), **sleep** (Monteleone, 1949), **space** (Monteleone, 1949), or **bullet** (Ross, *Behind Bars*, 2002).

A two-year sentence: **deuce** (Ersine, 1933) or the poorly spelled **duce** (Monteleone, 1949).

A five-year sentence: **five-spot** or **V** (Ersine, 1933), **fin** or **finif** (Monteleone, 1949), or **nickel** (Burroughs, *Junkie*, 1953).

A five-to-ten-year sentence: **arm and a leg** (McNellis, 1991).

A five-to-fifteen-year sentence: **taxi** (Ersine, 1933).

A ten-year sentence: a **sawbuck** (Ersine, 1933) or a **dime** (Cooper, *The Farm*, 1967).

A twenty-year sentence: **double saw**, **double sawbuck** or **twenty spaces** (Monteleone, 1949).

A life sentence: **the book** (Ersine, 1933), **from now on** or **doing it all** (Monteleone, 1949), the **wheel** (McNellis, 1991), or **L** or **retired** (Ross, *Behind Bars*, 189, 193). Because **the book** is a life sentence, a **bookman** is a prisoner who is serving a life sentence (Monteleone, 1949).

Still in the vocabulary of sentences, a **catnap** (Ross, 2002) is a short sentence, a **garter** (Monteleone, 1949) is an undetermined sentence, **the limit** (Monteleone, 1949) is the maximum sentence for a crime, and **stiff rap** (Monteleone, 1949) or **Buck Rogers** (Ross, 2002) is a long sentence. A prisoner who has been sentenced to jail many times with brief intermissions in the free world is said to be **serving life on the installment plan** (Monteleone, 1949), while a prisoner who is serving consecutive sentences is said to be **pulling a train** (Ross, 2002).

CHAPTER 4

The Military

There are undoubtedly many who would be offended by the suggestion that the men and women who serve in the armed forces are oppressed, even if only for sociolinguistic purposes. Four factors support the suggestion, though, and the slang that emerges from members of the armed forces sings with the verve of the oppressed. The argument begins with the obvious—by definition and by necessity, the armed forces always have been, are, and always will be authoritarian institutions based on a stringent, unquestioned system of command and control. Orders are given by those who give orders and orders are followed by those who follow orders, no point between, no discussion, no debate, no vote, just obey. Secondly, layered on top of this autocratic regime is the undeniable fact that each branch of the armed forces is a large, unwieldy, and at-times completely inefficient, even bungling bureaucracy that at times resembles the antithesis of a meritocracy. Thirdly, until the last three major American wars (the Gulf War of 1991 and the invasions and occupations of Afghanistan and Iraq that began in 2002 and continue today), those serving in combat were in large part conscripts, meaning that the draft rendered the participation of many troops in a highly authoritarian institution involuntary. Lastly, in times of war the task of most members of the armed services is to kill others who are trying to kill them, which adds to the sense of coercion.

These factors combine to create a dynamic that may not precisely fit the definition of oppression and may not justify a geometric boast of *QED, or quod erat demonstrandum*, but it comes close enough to the prison model of oppression to explore, especially in the wars fought before President Nixon ended the draft on January 27, 1973, in favor of an all-volunteer army.

In response to this oppression, what is the young recruit or conscript to do? Overt resistance is nearly unheard of in the American armed forces. To be sure, there are instances of mutiny in American military history. In June 1783, several hundred soldiers in the Continental Army took part in a mutiny that became known as the Pennsylvania Line Mutiny or Philadelphia Mutiny. There were several racially-motivated mutinies during World War II, in which African-American soldiers and sailors balked at racial discrimination—Bamber Bridge (June 23–24, 1943), Camp Van Dorn (Fall, 1943), Fort Devens (March 10, 1944), Brooklyn Field (May 24, 1944), Camp Claiborne (August 16, 1944), Port Chicago (August, 1944), the Tuskegee Airmen at Freeman Field (April 5, 1944), and Port Hueneme (March, 1945). During the late stages of active American participation in the Vietnam War, African-American sailors staged a mutiny onboard the USS *Constellation* (June, 1972) over perceived racial discrimination by the ship's commanders.

Despite the glamour and romance of collective defiance, these rare instances of open insubordination breathe new life into the meaning of Alinsky's "pointless sure-loser confrontation." Acts of everyday resistance must suffice, and within the arsenal of everyday resistance is slang. Combat fuels a resentment of authority and a dislike of regimentation, while fostering a strong sense of egalitarianism. The slang that soldiers have coined reflects these values. Their slang is imaginative and largely unsentimental, seeking ground a pole away from self-pity. It is blunt, unaffected, and what it lacks in social graces it gains by irony and dry humor.

Embracing the suck—a grunt—and proud of it

As is the case with other oppressed groups, members of the armed forces use slang to construct a positive, collective identity, communal values, and solidarity. If one accepts the premise that members of the armed services are oppressed, then there is no more oppressed group than the soldiers of the infantry. They live under the roughest and most challenging of conditions, are most prone to becoming casualties, and until recent wars were largely draftees, fighting involuntarily. As the most oppressed of the oppressed, their language is of the greatest interest.

In the spirit of "everything they say we are, we are, and we are very proud of ourselves" (Jefferson Starship) or "embrace the suck" (Iraq war), infantrymen have not gilded or glorified their role—they accept and relish their lowly status. The one word used by infantry soldiers to describe themselves that most embodies the use of slang to construct a positive identity is **grunt** (1962).

Without warning, in the early years of the Vietnam War along came **grunt** (1963), a term that had since 1926 been applied to an unskilled member of an electric or telephone line crew who works on the ground, almost certainly derived from the German *grund* (ground). By 1942 it was recorded as meaning any menial laborer, yet in the Army Signal Corps, it continued in the specialized sense to refer to a groundman on telephone line crew through World War II. When **grunt** moved from the groundman on an electric crew to an infantryman, it is not clear if the previous sense with its German was the genesis or whether it represented the primal sound made by infantrymen marching or in combat. Whether it imported its German heritage or simply meant to embody the low, gruff sounds made by an infantry soldier (a theory embraced by many ignorant of the original etymology), the term grabbed hold and would not let go.

※ ※ ※

Clark was actually more of "**grunt**" than an aviator.
    —Richard Tregaskis: *Vietnam Diary* (1963) 401

He is a crunch or **grunt** (terms applied to riflemen and taken from the sounds of soldiering—the crunch of boots and grunts of struggle.)
    —*Ebony Magazine* (August 1968) 38

They had fought their way up Hills 21 and 22, seeing
Viet Nam only through their rifle sights, living the daily
desperation of the infantry **grunt**.
　　　　—Hugh A. Mulligan: *No Place to Die* (1967) 305

In Southeast Asia, "**grunt**" is GI slang for a frontline
soldier. (The term comes from the grunting sound foot
soldiers make while carrying heavy packs.)
　　　　—House Committee on Armed Services:
　　　　　Extension of the Draft (1971) 687

　Even in an all-volunteer army there are infantry soldiers, and despite
the end of selective service and conscription, **grunt** made the leap to the
all-volunteer forces and usages abound in accounts of the Gulf War as
well as the invasions and subsequent military occupations of Afghanistan and Iraq:

❇ ❇ ❇

"In Texas, the economy is really bad. I have no real
skill. I'm a **grunt**, maybe a little smarter than your
average **grunt**, but what can I do?"
　　　　—Ray Tessler: "The Marines are shedding a few
　　　　　good men," *Los Angeles Times* (December 8,
　　　　　1991), B1

"That's all our agenda is, the well-being of the **grunts**
who are on the bloody end of the spear—the ones
kicking in doors in Falujah, driving convoys from
Baghdad to Basra and freezing on the plains in
Afghanistan."
　　　　—Brigid Shulte: "Doing Battle for the Grunts,"
　　　　　Washington Post (February 9, 2006) T03

For Kevin, this all makes sense, becoming a Marine
infantryman, rifleman, door-kicker, **grunt**. Choose
your term. This is what he has wanted to do for years.

Many of his friends went to college. Kevin is going to
Afghanistan.
　　—Frank Davies: "My son the Marine heads off
　　to war," *San Jose Mercury News* (July 2, 2009)

Before **grunt** came on the scene, the infantry soldier was known as a
doughboy (1867), a term most commonly associated with the American Expeditionary Forces during World War I. The term's etymology is
subject to conjecture—another way of saying "unknown." In *Army Talk*,
Elbridge Colby presents four equally unlikely/likely explanations, and
then invites the reader to "choose for yourself." Examples of its usage
abound:

⠶ ⠶ ⠶

Oh I want to be a **doughboy** / Doughboy tried and true /
I want to be a doughboy / With hat cord of baby blue.
　　—Plattsburgh Military Training Camp:
　　Rookie Rhymes (1917) 118

Imagine the confusion and mix up as tooth brushes,
soap, knives, spoons and forks scattered through the
straw as forty packs were unrolled. Oh, the life of a
doughboy.
　　—Frank Alexander Holden: *War Memories*
　　(1922) 63

On his feet, the **doughboy** will wear knee-length laced
boots of tan leather.
　　—*Popular Science* (April 1935) 7

Johnny **Doughboy** found a rose in Ireland / Sure the
fairest flow'r that Erin ever grew / Of the Glarney in
her talk / Took him back to Old New York / Where his
mother spoke the sweetest blarney too.
　　—Kay Twomey and Al Goodhart: *Johnny
　　Doughboy Found a Rose in Ireland* (1942)

Although the term remained understood in World War II, as reflected in the 1942 popular song *Johnny Doughboy*, it was gradually supplanted by **dog face** (1930) and **doggie** (1937).

⠿ ⠿ ⠿

How are you, old **dog face**? I knew your outfit was around here somewhere.
> —Terry Bull: *Sergeant Terry Bull* (1943) 37

If there is one thing a **dogface** loves, it is artillery—his own.
> —Audie Murphy: *To Hell and Back* (1949) 58

It hurts the **doggies** to see a man starting glassily at the shambles of the home he spent his life building.
> —Bill Maudin: *Up Front* (1945) 69

I watch those brave **doggies** die trying to attack.
> —Ernest Spencer: *Welcome to Vietnam,*
> *Macho Man* (1967) 135

Moving to the lesser planets, there is a series of terms that build on the infantryman's feet and legs—the almost-conventional **foot army** (1702), **blister foot** (1943), **footslogger** (1943), **straight leg** (1951), **leg** (1964), and **lego** (1971).

⠿ ⠿ ⠿

"We would rather have a highly mechanized, relatively small army than a large ill-equipped **foot army**," he said.
> —Ramananda Chatterjee (editor): *The Modern*
> *Review* (1951) 6

Infantrymen earned the nickname "**blisterfoot**."
> —Sylvia Whitman: *Uncle Sam Wants You!* (1993) 35

Nothing pleased the **foot slogger** struggling in the mud
of Italy more than hearing that Eisenhower had put
Spaatz or some other general in his place.
      —Stephen Ambrose: *The Supreme Commander*
      (1999) 321

He related that, after returning from months in the
bush on a mission, he was interviewed by an Army
"straight-leg" general.
      —Fred Edwards: *The Bridges of Vietnam* (2001) 98

Airborne, **"straight leg,"** which is best? / AIRBORNE!
AIRBORNE! Yes, Yes, Yes.
      —Sandee Shafter Johnson: *Cadences* (1986) 91

We sit around practicing with the guns while the **"legs"**
walk all day.
      —David Parks: *GI Diary* (1968) 37

Lego. Infantry unit.
      —Ronald J. Glasser: *365 Days* (1971) 243

Another set of names for the soldier in the infantry consist for the
most part of compound nouns built on their relationship with the earth
over which they trod and fight. They include **gravel agitator** (1898),
gravel crusher (1901), **ground pounder** (1942), **mud crusher** (1895),
crunchy (1951), **dust-biter** (1991), **janitor** (1991), **bullet stopper** (1991),
and **dirt eater** (2005).

░░ ░░ ░░

He insisted that the term doughboy, as applied to a
gravel agitator, had not originated in the Philippines,
as some alleged.
      —Alfred Comebise: *The Stars and Stripes* (1984) 103

God, who would've thought that plain **gravel-crushers**
like us would ever get rich pickin's like this.
      —Charles Harrison: General Die in Bed (1930) 232

Ground-to-air communications were essential to make sure both pilot and **groundpounder** knew what direction the plane would be coming from.
>—James Carafano: *GI Ingenuity, improvisation, technology* (2006) 151

MUD CRUSHERS. Very old army slang for the infantry. Descriptive, like **"gravel crushers,"** but usually derisive.
>—Elbridge Colby: *Army Talk* (1942) 141

Armed helicopters were especially reassuring to the **"crunchies,"** the ground infantrymen who depended on them to deliver accurate supporting fire.
>—Shelby Stanton: *The Rise and Fall of an American Army* (1985) 86

Its soldiers rode into battle in Bradleys and often called themselves **"crunchies,"** "grunts," or "11 Mikes" in reference to their Military Occupation Specialty— 11 M, meaning mechanized infantryman.
>—John McManus: *The 7th Infantry Regiment* (2008) 176

A **dust-biter** would ask a pogue if he ever set up a T.R. double E—referring to an antenna—and the pogue would almost always say "Yes."
>—E. M. Flanagan: *Lightning: The 101st in the Gulf War* (1994) 234

Janitor Infantry soldier, one without special skills, as distinguished from communication or transportation specialists.
>—*American Speech* (Winter 1991) 392

Bullet-stoppers. The U.S. Navy's term for the Marines.
>—"GI's come up with their own Gulf Lingo," *New York Post* (February 9, 1991) 3

For good reasons, soldiers called a light weapons infantryman (whose MOS was an 11-B), an 11-**Bullet-stopper**.
　　—Peter Maslowski: *Looking for a Hero* (2005) 164

The last had been on special assignment for the Criminal Investigative Division, but the first two had been as a **dirt-eater** with the Twenty-fifth infantry.
　　—Thomas Holland: *KIA* (2008) 10

　Last and least are the rodent names, **boonie rat** (1967) for an infantry soldier assigned to a remote location, **tunnel rat** (1967) **ferret squad** (1982), and **house mouse** (1989), all referring to soldiers who searched and destroyed enemy tunnels.

##

When the hard-core **Boonie Rat** returns home from a tour in Vietnam, he has no qualms whatever about telling it like it is.
　　—Don Pratt: *Salmagundi Vietnam* (1970) 11

While it is generally known that the term **"tunnel rat"** refers to soldiers in Vietnam who search and destroy the Viet Cong tunnels, few people know much about the typical Viet Cong tunnel.
　　—Society of American Military Engineers: *The Military Engineer* (1967) 243

I remember once there were several people in the tunnel and we sent down two VC defectors in front of our **tunnel rat**.
　　—Jonathan Schell: *The Military Half* (1968) 37

Ferret squads. Soldiers whose specialty is tunnel and house-to-house fighting.
　　—Frank Hailey: *Soldier Talk* (1982) 22

Every Company had what they called their "**house mouse**," who was usually the smallest guy in the bunch.
—*Houston Chronicle* (October 17, 1989)

The same embrace of the lowly drives the infantryman's choice of verb for what he does most. An infantry rifleman marches, a grunt **humps** (1971). There is no sugar-coating, no glaze, just the brutal reality of what it is he does—carry and march a heavy pack and weapons. The term may have been used somewhat in Korea, especially in the context of "humping the Yamas" for patrolling the DMZ, as recorded by Frank Hailey (1982), but it was a quintessentially Vietnam War word, blunt, unsentimental, ironic, and proud.

▓ ▓ ▓

"We were out **humping** the boonies (patrolling) when the pointman got hit and he was laying out there wounded and we were trying to get to him.
—Mark Jury: *The Vietnam Photo Book* (1971) 102

"Four deuce beats **humpin'** the boonies."
—William Penfry: *The Big V* (1972) 6

"**Hump**," "humping," and "humping the boonies" were the soldiers' terms for long and exhausting marches over rugged jungled-covered terrain.
—George Moss: *Vietnam: An American Ordeal* (1990) 186

The verb form converts to noun form in the compounds **paddy humping** (1978) for marching through rice paddies and **hill humper** (1967) for an infantryman.

▓ ▓ ▓

It didn't take long for me to master the secret of **paddy humping**.
—Larry Gwin: *Baptism: A Vietnam Memoir* (1999) 33

> In Vietnam, he goes by an assortment of names—the
> Grunt, Boonie Rat, Line Dog, Ground Pounder, **Hill
> Humper**, or Jarhead.
> > —David Reed: *Up Front in Vietnam* (1967) 3

Throughout, the lowly, despised infantryman embraces the hand that he has been dealt and, resorting again and again to dysphemism, bluntly coins language that proclaims pride in the arduous, dangerous job of an infantryman.

Terms with which to disparage: from REMF to Fobbit

Having used slang to reinforce their own identity, members of the armed forces next turn to slang to disparage those who, one way or another, are responsible for their oppression and suffering. Mocking, ridiculing, and denigrating authority is an important function of slang for the oppressed, and thus it is in the military.

It would seem intuitive that recruits and conscripts would scorn all officers as symbols of authority, but this is not the case, at least not to the degree that might be expected. While many slang terms gently mock officers, they are largely free of bite and sting.

Just as prisoners sometimes refer to their warden as the **old man** (1830), members of the armed forces will use the term to describe their commanding officer, combining affection and derision in a single phrase. The term is most commonly used in the Navy, but is heard in land forces as well:

⠿ ⠿ ⠿

> The **old man** gave the order to move. And baby, we
> moved. Our tracks hit the jungle blasting with full fire
> power.
> > —David Parks: *GI Diary* (1984) 51

> There was a lifer in San Diego who was dumped for
> indebtedness. The **old man** got sick of the dunning
> letters so he had the man discharged and thereby made
> the matter a non-navy problem.
> > —David Ponicsan: *The Last Detail* (1970) 13

The most common slang term for officers in general is **brass** (1899), a mild mocking of the importance placed by officers on the brass symbols of authority.

⠿ ⠿ ⠿

Secretary of Defense Donald Rumsfeld won the first argument about the size of the invasion force; it was far smaller than Army **brass** wanted.
—*Chicago Tribune* (April 8, 2004) C24

In Afghanistan, the army **brass** saw the media coverage as one of the biggest dangers to their career.
—Andrew Exum: *This Man's Army* (2004) 199

Joining **brass** and its gentle tease of brass insignia worn by officers are a number of quasi-derisive terms used by common fighting men to mock the awards and ribbons worn by officers. In 1942, Elbridge Colby recorded **crow tracks** in *Army Talk*, while in 1982 Frank Hailey recorded **butter sticks**, **fruit salad**, **goldies**, and **scrambled eggs**.

The tease gives way to scorn when it comes to officers freshly arrived in combat after brief training at Officer Candidate School. The combination of elitism and inexperience is deadly in the eyes of the enlisted man, who has referred to these newly coined officers as **90-day wonders** (1917) or, in homage to quick dinner preparation techniques, **shake-and-bake** (1977).

⠿ ⠿ ⠿

The soldiers were just finishing bivouac overseas when a young **90-day wonder** lieutenant walked up to the colored soldier and said, "Soldier where is my foxhole?"
—*Ebony Magazine* (August 1968) 108

The author, a graduate of the Navy's accelerated three-month training program—a "**90-day wonder**"—was assigned to command the central control ship.
—*The Rotarian Magazine* (December 1990) 52

In my opinion, some of the problem stemmed from the
"shake and bake" promotion system of the late 1960s
and early 1970s.
—John Moellering: *Battalion Commanders Speak
Out* (1977)

A twenty-year-old **Shake 'n' Bake** sergeant by the
name of Larry Closson had just arrived with a new
batch of cherries.
—Larry Chambers: *Recondo* (1992) 87

The recruit or conscript is totally unforgiving of those stationed far
from battle and danger. The greatest scorn in the soldier's slang vocabulary is reserved for those in service but not in combat. For the soldier in
Vietnam, **remf** (1973), short for "rear-echelon motherfucker," was the
ultimate disparagement.

⚔ ⚔ ⚔

I learned that **REMF** means "rear echelon
motherfucker"; that a man is getting "short" after his
third or fourth month; that a hand grenade is a "frag."
—Tim O'Brien: *If I Die in a Combat Zone* (1973) 76

A **REMF** is a rear-echelon motherfucker, one of those
useless, order-generating bastards who gets us line-
animals killed.
—Tom Clancy: *Clear and Present Danger* (1990) 617

It's **REMF**, pronounced **REMF**, and it stands for Rear
Echelon Mother Fucker, something you ain't as of now.
—Dale Dye: *Platoon* (1987) 9

Soldiers in Iraq have gradually dropped **remf** in favor of **fobbit,** but
not without first coining a new name for the rear echelon—**remfland**
(2007).

I knew the General would be after my ass in the morning if not the MP's tonight. Oh well, life in the "**remf-land**" still sucks!

—Kelly Beckman: *The Boomers* (2008) 258

Another common put-down word for rear-echelon support personnel is **pog** or **pogue** (1972), which made it from Korea to Vietnam to Iraq. Some argue that it is an acronym for "Person Other Than Grunt," but this is almost certainly back formation from a term that had earlier (1919) been applied to a young man playing the passive role in a homosexual relationship.

When the engineers are picking up mines ahead of the infantry we're great men but when they catch us with picks and shovels back on a supply road we're **pogues.**

—Bill Mauldin: *Bill Mauldin in Korea* (1952) 127

It was the ages-old animosity between front-line infantrymen and the staff and support personnel farther back—the "**pogues**," "those rear-echelon motherfuckers!" Those who wrote the op orders never had to carry them out.

—Charles Robert Anderson: *The Grunts* (1976) 38

First of all, I'm a grunt. I'm very proud of that. I had two tours in Iraq. I can't honestly say that I never bad mouthed a **pog** (pogue for all you older vets). I didn't make it into a hobby as some of my colleagues did. I knew that they were needed and that they were important to mission success. I don't agree with the all-or-nothing definition some ignorant grunts use for pogs.

—50CallExtrordinaire:http://militarytimes.com/forum (11/21/08)

Taking the place of **remf** in the language of scorn for those removed from combat is **fobbit** (2004), The term is based on the acronym FOB (forward operating base) and then joins forces with "hobbit."

⠿ ⠿ ⠿

"If they take one step further off the fob, it's the furthest they've ever gone," Ferrell says. For **fobbits,** deployment is a lot like life in the States, only they wear uniforms and occasionally carry weapons—and the food, courtesy of Halliburton, is actually better.
    —David Axe: "The Dread Zone," *The Village Voice* (March 1, 2005), 36

You might call them admin weenies and **fobbits,** but don't shoot at the human resources specialists. They're trained to shoot back—and do.
    —Gina Cavallaro: "Every Admin Soldier a Rifleman," *Army Times* (October 3, 2005) 20

Over the years, there have been dozens of derisive epithets for those removed from the field of battle yet directing the battle, including **stateside commando** (1947), **Saigon warrior** (1969), **chairborne** (1982) punning on "Airborne," **headquarters puke** (1986), and **perfumed prince** (2006).

⠿ ⠿ ⠿

Why the heck you picked a **stateside commando** for the cover has got me.
    —*Air Force Magazine* (1954) 78

My first weeks in Vietnam provided me with a quickly fleeting view of what life had been like for the **Saigon Warrior**.
    —John Steinbeck: *In Touch* (1969) 9

You see, my dear sons, I was a "**Saigon Warrior**."
    —Jan Vanderbie: *Prov Rep Vietnam* (1970) 103

Inouye, a leader in the Army's most decorated combat unit, the Nisei 442nd Regimental Combat Team, was recommended for the Medal of Honor, a proposal that subsequently was knocked down a notch at headquarters, a not-uncommon practice in the **chairborne** military.
> —Gus Stevens: "Inouye Helping to Make Hearings Great Daytime TV," *San Diego Union-Tribune* (July 22, 1987) C7

I'm a **headquarters puke**—Just look at me!
> —Sandee Johnson: *Cadences* (1986) 108

Some **headquarters puke** decided to downgrade it, reason unknown.
> —Tom Clancy: *The Teeth of the Tiger* (2004) 224

Charles said he came to his own conclusion that the **"perfumed princes"** of the Pentagon did not have the best interest of the grunts at heart when he was training replacement Marines to go to Vietnam in 1968 at Camp Pendelton in California.
> —Brigid Schulte: "Doing Battle for the Grunts," *Washington Post* (February 9, 2006) T03

From vomit to perfume—quite an array of derision of those who risk little by those who risk all, everyday resistance to the personification of oppression.

Situation Normal – FU Beyond All Recognition

The inefficiency, incompetence, and waste sometimes displayed by the armed forces is the core of much military humor. Until the 143rd and final episode of *The Phil Silvers Show,* the wily Master Sergeant Ernest G. Bilko outsmarted the over-his-head, incompetent commander of the fictitious Fort Baxter in fictitious Roseville, Kansas. The ridiculous nature of Army regulations and procedures and the clash between draftees and uncaring, inept military leadership were the central unifying themes of the long-running television comedy *M*A*S*H*, set in a Mobile Army Surgical Hospital in Uijeonbu, South Korea, during the Korean War. No work skewered the absence of logic in the military more brilliantly than Joseph Heller's *Catch-22*, a dark comedy set during World War II, humorously pitting conscripts against a military establishment epitomizing incompetence. A bungled state of affairs, fairly or not, is the cornerstone and central theme of most military humor.

Through slang, the common soldier, sailor, and airman decry the absurdity and idiocy of the authority that controls their lives. The word "fuck" entered the vocabulary of American soldiers in World War I but really found its feet during World War II, and it came in handy for describing bureaucratic bungling. "Fuck," in the sense that "fucked up" means bungled or in disarray, formed the foundation of two critically important pieces of military slang, the acronyms **SNAFU** ("situation normal, all fucked up," first recorded in 1941), and **FUBAR** ("fucked up beyond all recognition," first recorded in 1944). The word "fuck" remained scandalous in polite society, and so "fouled up" was often used instead until the late 1960s when "fucked up" began to regularly appear in print as the meaning of "FU." There were dozens of subsequent pretenders built upon the "FU" construction, but none had the lasting power of **SNAFU** and **FUBAR**, which so simply and elegantly articulate the common soldier's view of life in the military.

⠶ ⠶ ⠶

And it was more than a "**snafu**" tolerance test, for it afforded insight into the candidate's range of affective behavior as well as the security measures which he took against anxiety.
   —United States Office of Strategic Services: *Assessment of Men* (1948) 111

Situation normal, all fucked up. Peter applied to officers' candidate school, and was rejected: eyesight not good enough, though adequate to fire an M-1 rifle.
   —Gore Vidal: *Washington D.C.* (1967) 132

The superlative of **SNAFU** is **FUBAR**. To be **FUBAR**
is much worse. It means, Fouled Up Beyond All
Recognition. Well, Italy was beyond **SNAFU**; it was
FUBAR.
>—Richard Lardner Tobin: *Invasion Journal* (1944) 48

FUBAR translated into "Fucked Up Beyond All
Recognition."
>—Ralph G. Martin: *The G.I. War* (1967) 9

Less profane but equally disdainful at the two most common names for
the Pentagon, the headquarters of the Department of Defense in Arling-
ton, Virginia—the **puzzle palace** (1956) and **Disneyland East** (1962).

☷ ☷ ☷

It was almost a daily occurrence to have people from
the **"puzzle palace"** call.
>—Edward J. Ruppelt: *The Report on Unidentified*
>   *Flying Objects* (1956) 193

Now, the Pentagon was being called "Fort Futility,"
"The Puzzle Palace."
>—James W. Canan: *The Superwarriors* (1975) 3

Mr. Flood: Since they are now beginning to refer to the
Pentagon as **"Disneyland East."**
>—House Committee on Appropriations:
>   *Department of Defense Hearings* (1962) 125

But all those critical labels—**Disneyland East**, the
Marbled Jungle, the Citadel.
>—Kenneth Lasson: *Private Lives of Public Servants*
>   (1978) 62

The term **Disneyland East** was apparently coined by Mort Sahl several
years earlier (1960), who used it in reference to Cape Canaveral.

Similar scorn and contempt for an organization that armed its fighters poorly can be found in the term **idiot stick** (1962) meaning a rifle, **Mattel toy rifle** (1986) and **widow-maker** (recorded in 1990 by Gregory Clark: *Words of the Vietnam War*) for the sometimes unreliable M-16 rifle, and **hillbilly armor** (2004), used by desperate soldiers in Iraq who were improvising body and vehicle armor because the Department of Defense had failed to provide adequate protection for the soldiers sent to invade and occupy a hostile country with a robust insurgency.

❖ ❖ ❖

The insignia of the Infantry was crossed rifles, which people called "**idiot sticks**."
—Larry King: *Love Stories of World War II* (2007) 68

I state categorically that the "**Mattel toy rifle**" is not fit for a grown man to fight a war with.
—Ralph Zumbro: *Tank Sergeant* (1986) 94

Milican only briefly spoke of the "horrible sand," unrelenting heat, "**hillbilly armor**" they initially wore and camel spiders as big as a Frisbee.
—Deena Winter: "Chaplain Brings Message Back Home," *Bismarck Tribune* (August 30, 2004) 1A

"We call it '**hillbilly armor**' because all we did was cut out thick steel and put it on our doors," Jackson said. "We have a really good welder who worked really hard on that to give us the extra protection."
—Stephanie Heinatz: "Truck Drivers Recount the Road to Baghdad," (Newport News) *Daily Press* (September 11, 2004) A4

Finally, from the all-volunteer army occupying Iraq come two splendid pieces of advice for soldiers burdened by the bureaucracy and incompetence surrounding them: **embrace the suck** (recorded in 2007 by Austin Bay: *Embrace the Suck*) and **shut up and color** (posted on October 18, 2007, at http://www.motherjones.com/politics/2007/10/lexicon-iraq-war-lingo-fightin-words).

Time and Place

As is the case with prisoners, time is a critical issue to the soldier, sailor, or airman. The commitment to life in the armed forces, and in most cases the assignment to combat, is finite. During the term of the commitment, the armed forces exert nearly total control over the soldier's time, and so the passing of time until the end of the tour of duty is very important. As is the case with prison slang, military slang reflects the central role played by time and the need to affect with words something that actions cannot affect. Not surprisingly, there is a moderate amount of overlap when it comes to the terms used by prisoners and members of the armed forces when describing time.

During the Vietnam war, members of the armed forces were sent into combat for a prescribed period, 13 months for the Marines, 12 months for the other branches. The official name for the end of the tour of duty was Date of Expected Return from Overseas, or **DEROS**. For those fighting in Vietnam, the official acronym noun became a slang verb, and to **DEROS** (1968) was thus to leave combat duty in Vietnam.

※ ※ ※

George had managed to postpone getting **DEROS'd**
back to the States so he could stay with—what was her
name, anyway?
　　　—Andrew Kaplan: *Scorpion* (1986) 234

He would **DEROS** when the Green Man was through
with him which should be in as little as four days.
　　　—John M. Del Vecchio: *The 13th Valley* (1999)

I was a replacement for some other medic who had
either bought the farm or **DEROS'd**.
　　　—Daniel Evans: *Doc: Platoon Medic* (2002) 19

Waiting for the end of a combat tour to **DEROS** can be harrowing—and boring. American troops instantly seized upon the 1993 Bill Murray comedy *Groundhog Day* as a metaphor for life in a combat zone. Just as Bill Murray's character in the movie finds himself repeating the same day over and over again, members of the armed forces finding themselves repeating the same grinding monotony and fear over and over again quickly came to call life in a combat zone **Groundhog Day** (1993). Sailors on the aircraft carrier USS *America* (*U.S. News and World Report*, February 22, 1994), soldiers in Somali (Mark Bowden: *Black Hawk Down*, 1999), and President Clinton describing military life in Bosnia (*Remarks to American Troops at Tuzla Airfield, Bosnia-Herzegovina*, January 13, 1996) all used **Groundhog Day** as slang shorthand for an unpleasant situation that continually repeats. So, too, have soldiers in Iraq (*New York Times*, August 14, 2006). This modern use is unrelated to the historic use (asserted in 1982 by Frank Hailey in *Soldier Talk*, 29) in which the term referred to November 11, 1918, when the war ended and troops came out from the trenches in which they had been living and fighting and dying for months.

Like prisoners, enlistees and conscripts nearly the end of their term of duty describe themselves as **short** (1966), or **short-timers** (1968), both terms also used by prisoners.

⁂ ⁂ ⁂

"Three days and a wake up, and I'm home free. I'm getting **shorter** than your dick."
> —Charley Trujillo: *Dogs From Illusion* (1994) 183

He was initially shunned, but once he had settled in, the ticked-off days on his calendar were a constant reminder that he was getting "**short**," getting close to his departure date.
> —Penny Coleman: *Flashback; Posttraumatic Stress Disorder* (2007) 82

The sergeant arose languorously from his canvas cot
and with a grease pencil struck off another day on his
"short timer's calendar."
—Hugh A. Mulligan: *No Place to Die* (1967) 309

I'm getting short too. July 7, 1967 We got hit with
mortars and small arms last night. It's the third time in
two weeks. Dawley, another **short-timer**, got hit in the
arm, but he'll make it.
—David Parks: *Vietnamese Conflict* (1968) 124

Mitchell was a **short-timer** with 32 days to go before
return to the United States.
—Samuel Marshall: *West to Cambodia* (1968) 119

In the rear, everybody had a **short-timer's** calendar—
usually a Playboy foldout with the Bunny of the
Month divided up into numbered sections like a meat
company diagram of a beef cow or pig.
—Philip Beidler: *Late Thoughts on an Old War*
(2004) 15

The final morning on a combat tour of duty or of service was once
known as a **meatball** (recorded by Elbridge Colby in 1942 in *Army Talk*,
132), but in recent decades has been known by the same term which
had been used by prisoners—a **wake-up** (1950).

⚎ ⚎ ⚎

Sgt. Reasoner, in the ONE-TWO's hootch, announces
to his crew that he is getting out in 1 month, 2 days,
and a **wake-up**.
—*Hawaii Review* (1975) 33

"Just eight days and a **wake-up**." Wilson held up
his helmet and proudly showed the "short timers'
calendar."
—William Huggett: *Body Count* (1978) 365

As the end of a soldier's combat tour approaches, he develops an attitude embraced by the slang initialisms **FIGMO**—"Fuck it, got my orders," a term apparently coined during the post-war occupation of Japan. In Vietnam, infantrymen embellished the term and created **FIGMO charts** or carved **FIGMO sticks**, chronicling the days left in their tour of duty.

▓▓ ▓▓ ▓▓

> The watchmen have a succinct GI term for those who are about to go home. It is "**figmo**," which in polite, free translation means, "Farewell, I got my orders."
> —*Air Force Magazine* (1957) 56

> He was always waiting now, each day of his tour carefully marked on the **FIGMO chart** that was taped behind the door of his wall locker.
> —Courtland Bryan: *P.S. Wilkinson* (1965) 3

In Iraq, America's all-volunteer army has coined a new slang initialisms expressing the same sentiment—**KMAG—YO-YO**, short for "kiss my ass good-bye, you're on your own." (October 18, 2007, at http://www.mother jones.com/politics/2007/10/lexicon-iraq-war-lingo-fightin-words).

Finally is the trip home. The airplane taking a soldier back to the United States from Vietnam came to be known by the soldiers as a **Freedom Bird** (1968), a term that survived 40 years and several wars to reappear in the Gulf War and then again in the invasion of Iraq.

▓▓ ▓▓ ▓▓

> BIEN HOA, Vietnam. Seven of the eight Special Forces men cleared of murder charges boarded a "**Freedom Bird**" jetliner and took off for the United States.
> —*The Disgrunted Carpetbagger and Friends* (1968) 8

> There were a number of young airmen and soldiers, milling about in the terminal as they waited for the **Freedom Bird**.
> —*The Alcade Magazine* (March 1968) 6

MANAMA, Bahrain—Snapping salutes and slapping high-fives, the last known American prisoners of the Persian Gulf War were welcomed as heroes Wednesday after traveling from Baghdad to a U.S. Navy hospital ship. Meanwhile, U.S. paratroopers loaded their gear for their own "**freedom bird.**"
>—*St. Louis Post Dispatch* (March 7, 1991) 1A

The rest of the 4th Brigade began rolling in from their deployment to the war zone in November, with the last of them stepping off the **Freedom Bird** Saturday.
>—James Halpin: "Bittersweet Return," *Anchorage Daily News* (December 20, 2007) A1

The soldier in Vietnam returned from combat to **The World** or, using a slightly older term, **the land of the big PX.**

�֍ ✖ ✖

In Vietnam, the days of the week are the same, the seasons do not change; each man counts the days until he goes back to "**the world.**"
>—Senate Committee on the Judiciary: *Hearings* (1970) 6882

"Don't tell me, let me guess—You're th' guy who wuz due t' rotate back t' th' **world** prior to kisin' your orders."
>—Michael Hodgson: *With Sgt. Mike in Vietnam* (1970) 65

"I just can't hack it back in **the World**," he said.
>—Michael Herr: *Dispatches* (1977) 5

Samples of the new English: "**the land of the big PX,**" "no sweat," "goldbrick," and "goof-off."
>—Anthony Scarangello: *A Fulbright Teacher in Japan* (1957) 27

Kazuko has cut three records, has his own apartment,
wants to marry GI and live in **"Land of the Big Px."**
—*Ebony Magazine* (September 1967) 48

To men stationed out in the boonies, the United States
is the **Land of Big Px** and the All-Night Generator.
—Elaine Shepard: *The Doom Pussy* (1967) 72

"Lieutenant Castillo at this very moment is seeing that
it is loaded aboard the C-5 which will carry me to the
Land of the Big PX later today."
—W. E. B. Griffin: *By Order of the President* (2004) 134

The soldier in the Gulf War, not resting on Vietnam's laurels, coined a
new term for home—**Fort Living Room**, which was still around to be
used in the second invasion of Iraq twelve years later.

⁑ ⁑ ⁑

"How do you get 200 Iraqis into a phone booth?" "Tell
'em it's not theirs." "Where you from, soldier?" **"Fort
Living Room,"** says the bleary North Dakota National
Guardsman yanked from stability into a foxhole.
—Ed Offley: "Steeling for the Moment of Truth,"
Seattle Post-Intelligencer (February 4, 1991)

But pity the person who mistakes that jocularity for
laxity: Mess with his beloved Air Force and he'll issue
you a one-way ticket back to a destination he calls
"Fort Living Room."
—Kathleen O'Brien: "I am New Jersey,"
Star-Ledger (Newark) (November 23, 2008) 7

Chow

Military food, whether prepared in camp or packaged for field use,
is the brunt of endless humor to those inside and outside the military.
More importantly here, a healthy disrespect for it is a tie that binds
members of the armed forces, a common enemy, and an element of

military life that can be criticized without fear of reprisal—thus a perfect object for low-level resistance.

Soldiers, sailors, and aviators have an extensive, creative, and cynical vocabulary to describe their food. Starting with field rations, from 1940 until 1981 the individual, canned, pre-cooked rations for land forces were known as Type C or C-Rations. They were about what you would expect them to be, and their formal name gave rise to two slang terms that are more than just a little evocative of rodents—**c-rats** (1965) or simply **rats** (1976).

:: :: ::

His favorite kind of **C-rats** was turkey loaf—it was everybody's, it disappeared from the boxes quickly and tonight he was making do with boneless chicken.
—Harold Hayes: *Smiling Through the Apocalypse* (1969) 762

And one of the fun games that always went was you dropped the **C-rats** cans or the candy off the back of your truck.
—Vietnam Veterans Against the War: *The Winter Soldier Investigation* (1972) 36

Hey, Chief, Six says we're getting birds in with mail, **rats** and water. Hey man, fucking water!
—Charles Anderson: *The Grunts* (1976) 84

In 1981, the military introduced a new generation of lightweight field rations, the Meal-Ready-to-Eat, or MRE. The soldiers forced to eat the MRE's quickly came up with their own versions of what MRE stands for:

:: :: ::

In the old days the victuals were called C-rations. The Army now calls them MRE's: Meals-Ready-to-Eat. The soldiers call them **Meals-Rejected-by-Ethiopians**.
—Molly Moore: "Letter from Alaska," *Washington Post* (December 20, 1988) A3

Nutritious but boring; the GI's have dubbed them
"Meals Rarely Edible."
—Harry Levins: "Armor-Plated Words of War,"
St. Louis Post-Dispatch (January 20, 1991), 9A

Leaving the field, there is a seemingly endless slang vocabulary used to describe meals prepared in camp. Many of the terms could have been heard at the soda fountains or lunch counters back home, and their use in the field served, as they did at home, to reinforce social ties. Like any slang, military food slang terms are markers for club membership, and here the club is the "aren't we clever and funny boys" club. In this way, the slang builds a sense of community in the face of oppression (and terrible food). Many of the slang food terms further convey contempt for the food, adding another dimension to the function of the slang—raging against the hideous.

No term conveys the soldier's derision for the food served in camp than the well-known, long-loved **shit on a shingle** (1951) or **S.O.S.** for creamed beef or ground beef with gravy, served on toast.

⁘ ⁘ ⁘

If they were going into action, why couldn't it be something good, like fried eggs or pancakes and syrup? But that was the army for you. **Shit on a shingle.**
—Saul Levitt: *The Sun is Silent* (1951) 15

Chow was **S.O.S., shit-on-a-shingle**, ground beef and gravy slopped across a slice of bread.
—Thomas Berger: *Crazy in Berlin* (1958) 135

"What are you giving them, Sergeant?" "**Shit on a shingle**, Captain." "Christ, haven't we anything else?
—Noel Clad: *Love and Money* (1959) 414

The term was too good to stay in the military. It quickly spread to many different institutional settings, most prominently prison.

Moving beyond **shit on a shingle**, *Leatherneck Lingo: Presenting a Glossary of Marine Corps Slang* was published in 1942 by the editors of *The Chevron*, a weekly newspaper published by the Marines in the San Diego area. It included a full section on "Table Talk," which included the following food slang: **armored heifer** (canned milk), **cackleberries** (eggs), **collision mats** (pancakes), **fish-eyes** (tapioca), **goldfish** (canned salmon), **grass** (salad), **Jamoke** or **Joe** (coffee), **popeye** (spinach), **punk** (bread), **red lead** (catsup), **sea dust** (salt), **sea-going turkey** (fish), **seagull** (chicken), **side arms** (cream and sugar), **sinkers** (doughnuts), **slum** (stew), **target paste** (creamed chipped beef), and **worms** (spaghetti).

Also in 1942 Elbridge Colby published *Army Talk*, including these additional food terms: **army strawberries** (prunes), **battery acid** (coffee), **blood** (catsup), and **canned Willie** (corned beef hash).

Paul Dickson's 1978 "Gob Glossary" in *Chow* adds **albatross** (chicken), **armored cow** (condensed milk), **army chicken** (beans and frankfurters), **axle grease** (butter), **bags of mystery** (sausage), **Baltimore steak** (calf liver), **black soup** (coffee), **buzzard** (chicken or turkey), **canned cow** (condensed milk), **cat beer** (milk), **depth bombs** (eggs), **dog food** (corned beef hash), **eyewash** (garnishes), **fowl balls** (chicken croquettes), **gedunks** (sweets), **goo** (hash), **hand grenade** (hamburger), **ink** (coffee), **Irish grapes** (potatoes), **Irish turkey** (corned beef), **kennel rations** (meat loaf), **machine oil** (syrup), **monkey meat** (tough beef), **rabbit food** (salad), **red paint** or **red-eye** (catsup), **repeaters** (sausage), **salt horse** (salted beef), **Sammy** (syrup), **sand** (sugar), **sea cow** (condensed milk), **sea dust** (salt), **snake eyes** (tapioca), **sweep seed** (rice), **tin cow** (condensed milk), **tire patch** (pancake), and **weevil** (rice).

A final list of terms is found in Frank Hailey's 1982 *Soldier Talk*: **bale of hay** (Shredded Wheat™ cereal), **bug juice** (a sweet, powdered fruit-flavored drink), **Dalmation pudding** (rice and raisin pudding), **flat tires** (pancakes), **hen fruit** (eggs), **Irish ice cream** (mashed potatoes), **rocket fuel** (Texas chili), **tube steak and pearls** (frankfurters and beans), and **violets** (onions or garlic).

Overt Resistance

While overt resistance to military authority by members of the armed forces is rare, it is not entirely absent. As is the case with prisoners, members of the armed forces have constructed a slang vocabulary to describe the methods by which they subvert oppression. Rather than use the oppressor's language to describe what their brothers in arms are doing, they use their own slang lexicon.

Rumor and gossip is a low-level form of everyday resistance, and it is a weapon of the soldier, referring to such acts of public anonymity as a **latrine rumor** (1918) or **latrinogram** (1982 in Frank Hailey: *Soldier Talk*, 38). Through anonymous whispers, the invincibility of the oppressing force is whittled down.

⠿ ⠿ ⠿

Latrine rumor had said so many things, good, bad, and fantastic, that the wise guys had grown skeptical.
—Dixon Wecter: *When Johnny Comes Marching Home* (1944) 257

The **latrine rumor** keeps moving down the line. The man who was at the table talked to his friend. I have never seen anything spread so fast.
—Senate Committee on Armed Services: *Uniform Code of Military Justice Hearings* (1949) 90

Upon returning to our units, we passed around the information, whereupon someone would ask where we heard it. "It's a **latrine rumor**" was the usual reply.
—Roger Hayes: *On Point* (2001) 24

Another act of public anonymity that can used as a gesture of resistance is graffiti. A similar phenomenon occurred in Vietnam, the letters **FTA** for "fuck the army" (1963) painted on walls or soldiers' helmets, usually accompanied by what seemed to fastidious officers to be scruffy dress. The identity of the actor is of course not shielded in the case of a painted helmet, and his intentions are easily understood.

⠿ ⠿ ⠿

"**FTA**, sir." "And what does **FTA** stand for, Specialist?" "The initials stand for "Fuck the Army."
—Thomas Doulis: *Path for our Valor* (1963) 36

> A military organization simply cannot function if
> the attitude toward it of so many of its members is
> epitomized by the letters **FTA** (fuck the army).
> —John Gellner: *Bayonets in the Street* (1974) 149

> Like mine, it will coincide with discharge from the
> army. In honor of this fact, he replaced his name tape
> with the initials **FTA**.
> —James P. Sloan: *War Games* (1976) 84

The term was catchy, and the anti-war movement was quick to seize it. During the war, Jane Fonda, Donald Sutherland, and others performed in anti-war coffee houses near military bases; the name of the show—**FTA**.

Subtle acts of passive aggression are another form of everyday resistance by members of the armed forces. Shirking work is a popular form of passive aggressive resistance, known in the military as **goldbricking** (1918). Because of the strong egalitarian streak found in the armed forces, the term has a derisive edge.

⚏ ⚏ ⚏

> Well, I'd better quit **goldbricking** and go improve my
> foxhole (seriously!) or brush my teeth, or something.
> —Bill Adler: *Letters from Vietnam* (1967) 94

> For the grunt the role model for the typical **"goldbrick"**
> was a REMF.
> —Gregory Clark: *Words of the Vietnam War*
> (1990) 202

> "He said they were **goldbricking**," said Elizabeth Finn.
> "Some of these men were sick as dogs."
> —David Maraniss: *They Marched Into Sunlight*
> (2004) 468

Malingering and self-inflicting wounds are another form of passive-aggressive everyday resistance. Since Vietnam, American soldiers have referred to the **million dollar wound** (1905) or **million dollar zap** (1982 by Frank Hailey: *Soldier Talk*, 41)—a wound that is serious enough to preclude return to combat yet not serious enough to permanently disable the soldier. The term does not connote that the wound was self-inflicted, but it does express admiration for the soldier's luck in avoiding future combat.

:: :: ::

In the parlance of our camp, I had a "**million dollar wound**," which meant a long furlough with no danger to life or limb.
> —Alexander Hunter: *Johnny Reb and Billy Yank* (1905) 549

Seeing us, Snuffy hoists his buttocks in our direction and lovingly pats the large bloody bandage. "So long, you miserable sonsabitches," he yells. "I just got that **million-dollar wound**."
> —Audie Murphy: *To Hell and Back* (1949) 192

The surgeons came around to talk to Mansfield today and told him he had a **Million Dollar Wound**.
> —Richard Tregaskis: *Vietnam Diary* (1963) 22

It was a **million-dollar wound**, meaning there was no major structural damage so I should make a full recovery.
> —Clive McFarlane: "Obligation is fruit of family tree," *Worcester Telegram & Gazette* (November 3, 2006) B1

Petty theft is a type of everyday resistance that approaches, but does not reach the level of overt defiance. Far be it for the self-respecting soldier or sailor or airman to use the term "petty theft." Instead, the slang terms **liberate** (1944), **midnight requisition** (1946), and **moonlight requisition** (1946) are used with esteem and approbation.

✖ ✖ ✖

Brenda had said that they were stationed at Capua in an old fort, and they had **liberated** some beer and they wanted to give a little party for all of us.
　　　　—Margalo Gillmore: *The B.O.W.S.* (1945) 63

That sound like a good place to "**liberate**" some wine, and perhaps some silk stockings.
　　　　—Trevor Blore: *Comissioned Bargees* (1946) 133

The tank commander whipped out his pistol, which he had acquired by a "**midnight requisition**" and shot the Jap.
　　　　—National Rifle Association: *American Rifleman* (1944) 26

This was "**midnight requisition**" with a vengeance.
　　　　—Ralph Zumbro: *Tank Sergeant* (1988) 99

"One reason that I'm so happy to see you guys come in tonight is that we have to make a little **moonlight requisition** trip."
　　　　—Ralph Peterson: *Fly a Big Tin Bird* (2006) 70

The 92nd Airdrome Squadron excelled in its use of the **moonlight requisition**.
　　　　—Donald Anderson: *When War Becomes Personal* (2008) 84

Moving to the most overt acts of resistance, desertion is an option. One would imagine that desertion rates would plummet in an all-volunteer army, and this was in fact true until several years into the invasion and occupation of Afghanistan and Iraq. By 2007, the number of U.S. Army deserters had risen 80% since the invasion of Iraq began in 2003, reaching the highest rate in more than twenty-five years. Of course, no self-respecting soldier would say "desertion," they would say

French leave (1982 in Frank Hailey: *Soldier Talk,* 25) or, more commonly, they would use a term also used by prisoners and say that the deserter had **gone over the hill** (1912).

⠶ ⠶ ⠶

"I'm **going over the hill**. I've got it all figured out."
—Thomas Heggen: *Mister Roberts* (1946) 186

"But if he was against the Marine Corps, why didn't he do something about it? Like refuse an order. Or **go over the hill.**"
—Robert Stone: *Dog Soldiers* (1974) 207

The most extreme—and most dangerous—form of overt resistance is intentional fratricide. There are isolated instances in military history, but the practice of intentionally killing officers reached unprecedented levels in Vietnam. With the rise in intentional "friendly" killings came a new term, **frag** (1970) as the verb, and **fragging** (1970) as the noun. The term was derived from an earlier sense of **frag** (1943) as a fragmentary grenade, which was often the weapon of choice in killing officers who needlessly risked the lives of those under their command.

⠶ ⠶ ⠶

Montana was "**fragged**" to death as he lay sleeping in his billet at Bien Hoa.
—Jack McWethy: *The Power of the Pentagon* (1972) 24

The Pentagon reported 209 **fragging** incidents in 1970.
—James Clotfelter: *The Military in American Politics* (1973) 44

Take Care of Your Men. Some of the grunts showed themselves capable of still another negative act—the **fragging** of commissioned and non-commissioned officers.
—Charles Robert Anderson: *The Grunts* (1976) 187

Despite the all-volunteer nature of the army that invaded and occupies Iraq and Afghanistan, the rate of post-traumatic stress disorder diagnoses and suicides is alarmingly high. **Fragging**, however, is largely unknown in Iraq or Afghanistan. The term was often used in discussions of the 2004 "friendly fire" death in Afghanistan of former professional football star Pat Tillman, most notably by MSNBC commentator Chris Matthews on July 26, 2007.

※ ※ ※

We'll never know the true facts of that night skirmish
in Afghanistan, and we won't know the circumstances
of why he was in front of his squad. It could have been
confusion, heightened excitement, or even a **fragging**.
—Andree Mondor: *Courtier-Journal* (Lousiville),
Reader's Forum (August 27, 2007) 8A

Tillman was courage personified, and he did not brook easily the complaints or sniveling of his fellow soldiers. This, the theory goes, may have led to his killing.

CHAPTER 5

Also Oppressed . . .

Not every oppressed group in the United States uses slang as a means of resistance, but there are certainly other groups with slang vocabularies with elements of resistance. Homosexual men that are oppressed because of their sexuality, workers that are oppressed because of their class, Jews that are oppressed because of their immigrant status and religion, and Mexican Americans that are oppressed because of their ethnicity and immigrant status all use slang to some degree to register resistance to oppression. The resistance-driven lexicon is not as extensive with these groups as it is with African Americans, prisoners, and soldiers, but the basic characteristics expected in slang-as-resistance are present.

Gay Men

The oppression suffered by homosexual men and women is in significant ways different from oppression suffered by others. In some states, homosexuality is a legal basis for discrimination. Many organized religions vehemently and passionately denounce homosexuality and, of those, many denounce homosexuals. Politicians and conservative commentators publicly denounce homosexuals and their "homosexual agenda," using homosexuality as a wedge political issue. A homosexual may be despised by their own relatives, bringing the oppression into the bosom of the family, a person's supposed rock-solid support in life.

120

Of all the minorities in the United States, only the homosexual man or woman can be publicly maligned with impunity.

As is the case with other oppressed people, homosexuals use slang to rage against the machine, in this case, the homophobic machine. For the most part, the slang of homosexuals is the slang of homosexual men, not lesbians, a dynamic that is addressed in a following chapter. The language of gay men is flamboyant, flashy, gaudy, creative, and prolific. A great deal of their slang is slang for slang's sake, a reflection of the humor and ostentation that characterize the culture of gay men. For example, much of the lexicon is devoted to sex, directly or indirectly, a fact that should not surprise given the central role sex plays in the lives of at least younger gay men. Arguably the purely sex slang is itself a gesture of resistance. Much of it is deliberately vulgar, a sometimes characteristic of the slang of the oppressed. Body parts, body functions, body secretions, sexual proclivities, sexual fetishes, and sexual acts are all graphically depicted in gay slang. There are hundreds of coarse words in the vernacular of homosexual men, all sexual. To some extent, this is slang for slang's sake, and to some extent it is a linguistic reflection of the values of the homosexual culture—defying conventional norms.

To read resistance into all of gay slang would be to overplay a hand. Not all gay slang serves as a gesture of resistance, but some certainly does. To start, gay men use slang to construct a positive, collective identity, and no word is more important to this effort than the word **gay** (1941) itself.

Gay started as an insider-only word, used largely as innuendo. The Oxford English Dictionary presents several attestations of **gay** from the 1920s and 1930s, with the *caveat* that reading these uses of **gay** in the modern sense of "homosexual" may or may not be accurate. The first explicitly and definitively homosexual use of **gay** is in Gershon Legman's "The Language of Homosexuality" found in G. Henry's *Sex Variants* (1941). Legman's work, which is the earliest published study of American homosexual slang, cites **gay** as meaning homosexual, noting that the term is "used almost exclusively by homosexuals to denote homosexuality" (1167).

The term spilled from inside the relatively small **gay** community in the 1950s and 1960s, but did not assume flood proportions until the early 1970s, when mainstream America learned that "homosexual" was out and **gay** was in, just as they had learned to say "woman" instead of girl" and to say "black" instead of "Negro."

☷ ☷ ☷

Not all who call their flats in Greenwich Village "studios" are queer. Not all New York's queer (or, as they say it, "**gay**") people live in Greenwich Village.
—Jack Lait and Lee Mortimer: *New York Confidential* 1948 (65)

Now, you see, I always thought that being **gay** was about the most iconoclastic, minority thing there was.
—Bernard Wolfe: *The Late Risers* (1954) 213

"I heard from a girl friend it was a **gay** place." "What does the word '**gay**' mean to you?" "Homosexual."
—*San Francisco News* (December 20, 1954) 1

Some come on **gay** and want me to help them be men again.
—"Silverstein in Greenwich Village," *Playboy* (September 1960)

Gay: the acceptable term for homosexuals, male or female.
—*Screw* (October 12, 1970)

Also met other **gay** cats, had many talks with them.
—Jefferson Polard: *The Records of the San Francisco Sexual Freedom League* (1971)

Gay men and lesbians know this like they know that sunlight casts shadows, like night follows day.
—Donn Teal: *The Gay Militants* (1971) 161

Today, even those who characterize homosexuality as a lifestyle choice use the term "**gay** lifestyle," and even those who denounce homosexuality will use the term in their denouncements. Further yet, even those who feel called upon to deny fairly emphatic evidence of their homosexuality will use the term in their denial, as did then-Senator Larry Craig on August 28, 2007: "Let me be clear: I am not **gay**. I never have been **gay**."

Gay has been used to form any number of slang compound words, including **gay bar** (1953), **gay chicken** (1959) for a young homosexual male, **gaydar** (1982) for the ability of one homosexual to identify a stranger as homosexual, **gay ghetto** (1971), and **gayola** (1960) for police extortion of homosexuals.

Another leg supporting the construction of a positive group identity is the open acceptance of feminine nouns and pronouns used by gay men to describe each other. By openly embracing the feminine, gay men embrace and empower their character.

The most prominent of these feminine nouns is **queen** (1919). Legman rather stiffly defined a **queen** as "a male homosexual, especially one of the effeminate type, and a pedicant or fellator." The word has evolved to refer to a flamboyant, melodramatic, ostentatious homosexual, and is usually spoken with admiration.

❇ ❇ ❇

Old Jewish mothers never know when their sons
are faggots. They just miss it somehow. Out-and-out
screaming **queens**—mothers are never hip.
  —Lenny Bruce: *The Essential Lenny Bruce* (1967) 162

The screaming **queen** counters with, "Well, you're
screaming too!" "No, I'm not," I said, laughing at him.
  —Ethan Mordden: *Some Men Are Lookers*
   (1998) 238

A fabulous flaming **queen** called Miss Destiny swept
into my life.
  —John Rechy: *Beneath the Skin* (2004) 164

In 1941, Legman recorded **auntie** (an older homosexual), **girl** (an effeminate homosexual), **ma** (used before a person's name), **miss** (used before a person's name), **mother superior** (an older man who is openly homosexual), and **wife** (the more passive member of a homosexual couple). In 1949, *The Gay Girl's Guide: A Primer for Novices* (First Edition) added **daughter** (a man whom the speaker has introduced to homosexuality) and **sister** (a close friend but not a lover). The pronoun **she** is commonly used by homosexual men when speaking of another homosexual man, first recorded by the Johns Committee's official report to the Florida legislature in 1964, *Homosexuality and Citizenship in Florida*.

A final identity-affirming term is an homage to gay icon Judy Garland's character Dorothy in *The Wizard of Oz*—**friend of Dorothy** (1991). In Baum's original novel, the Cowardly Lion asserts that "Any friend of Dorothy must be our friend, as well." Thus it was with gay men, who used the term as insider code for homosexual.

⁂

> No longer did men have to use the cruising code one-liner, "Are you a **friend of Dorothy?**"
> —Mark Thompson: *Leatherfolk* (1991) 109

> More than twenty thousand fans filed past her (Garland's) coffin, many of them a "**friend of Dorothy**," code for "gay" in those preliberation days.
> —Jack Cashill: *What's the Matter With California* (2007) 278

Just as African Americans have turned the world upside with a series of slang terms where good is bad and bad is good, so too have homosexuals. The standard English meanings of "straight" are positive—direct and undeviating (1386), frank and honest (1530). To the homosexual, however, **straight** (1941) means heterosexual and is useful both as a judgment-free descriptor or as a term of some derision. In this sense, **straight** is not just borrowed from standard English, but it also gained new connotations from the slang of the counterculture of the 1960s, in which **straight** meant conventional, boring, mainstream.

※ ※ ※

Back in the days when I was first in the navy, I didn't
know a gay guy from a **straight** guy.
　　　—Willard Motely: *Let No Man Write My Epitaph*
　　　(1958) 210

The pool-playing dykes sit at tables in one corner away
from the juke-box, and the "**straights**" fill out the rest
of the bar.
　　　—Roger Gordon: *Hollywood's Sexual Underground*
　　　(1966) 18

Listen, asshole, what am I going to do? He's **straight**.
　　　—Matt Crowley: *The Boys in the Band* (1968) 32

One day he told me that if there was anything that
could make him go **straight**, it was me.
　　　—Jefferson Poland: *The Records of the San
　　　Francisco Sexual Freedom League* (1971) 46

Gay slang is used to some extent to express scorn for the oppressor, but not to the extent found in other oppressed groups. As an equal and opposite reaction to the clipped and disparaging **homo** (1922), gay slang labels heterosexuals **hetero** (1933) or even more clippedly **het** (1972).

※ ※ ※

Anyways, what's so special about being gay except a lot
of heartaches and headaches? **Heteros** don't brag about
the novels and paintings they've produced because they
go to bed with the opposite sex.
　　　—Eros: *The Homosexual Magazine* (February
　　　1953) 19

In Big D, do as the **heteros** do.
—Phil Andros (Samuel Steward): *Stud* (1966) 89

I'm sick of watching **hets** in angst, **hets** in love, **hets**
getting rich, **hets** dying. **Hets, hets, hets.** I am sick,
sick, sick of them.
—Karen X. Tulchinsky: *Love Ruins Everything*
(1998) 267

Perhaps the most effective and clever term used to disparage heterosexuality is to call a heterosexual a **breeder** (1979), a term that hisses
with scorn with very little effort.

***

"Hey, what does a **breeder** know?" Michael grinned.
"Where did you learn that word?" The light changed.
They proceeded with graceless caution across the
pebbly asphalt. "One of the guys at Perry's," replied
Brian. "He said that's what the faggots call us."
—Armistead Maupin: *Further Tales of the City*
(1982) 167

Such a foolish admission may risk their censuring you
as a **breeder**. In this society, heterosexual people are
called **breeders**.
—*Homosexuality and the Catholic Church* (1983) 26

"So we defy them, see?" "Them?" I asked. **"Breeders."**
—Ethan Mordden: *Everybody Loves You* (1988) 209

Homosexuals who are not comfortable with their own homosexuality
and who disparage and denigrate other homosexuals are scorned by the
gay community. A person who has not accepted their own homosexuality is said to be **in the closet**, while to make public the fact of another's
homosexuality is to **out** them.

❇ ❇ ❇

Perhaps Craig was secretly jealous of their ability to
be open and free about their sexual orientation. This
could also be said of Mark Foley and Ted Haggard. The
clinical term for this is "reaction formation," where a
person avoids one position by taking a polar opposite
position. For gay people it's called "being **in the closet**."
　　—"Repressed Sexuality Leads to Bad Acts,"
　　　The Arizona Republic (September 2, 2007)
　　　Opinions page 4

This controversial exposé targets politicians who
allegedly remain **in the closet** while pushing anti-gay
legislation. It contends lawmakers such as Senator
Larry Craig have displayed homophobia in public,
despite secret agendas in their personal lives.
　　—*The Burlington Free Press* (July 16, 2009)

Outrage accuses Crist of being **in the closet**, citing as
evidence articles written by the Broward New Times'
Bob Norman, which quoted men who claimed to have
had affairs with Crist.
　　—Rene Rodriguez: *The Miami Herald* (July 30,
　　　2009) G14

When in the mid-1960s Angelo d'Arcangelo's
Homosexual Handbook indiscreetly **outed** Hoover,
the FBI did pressure the publisher to remove the
embarrassing mention.
　　—Warren Johansson: *Outing* (1994) 86

Slang of the oppressed is often characterized by humor, creativity, and
double-meaning. The language and the wit behind the language of gay
men infuses their slang with all three, emphasis on arch double meaning.
In fact, there is even a term for a word or phrase with a double meaning denoting homosexuality, **hairpins** (1950), with **dropping hairpins**

as the most common construction, referring to hinting through innuendo that one is homosexual.

⁑ ⁑ ⁑

Keep your **hairpins** up, dearies. There's a "straight" inside.
> —Anthony James: *America's Homosexual Underground* (1965) 162

In the argot of the gay subculture, "**dropping hairpins**," meant dropping clues that one was homosexual.
> —Toby Marotta: *The Politics of Homosexuality* (1981) 77

Hippies

For a few years in the late 1960s and early 1970s, the hippie counterculture seized the imagination of America's young. The children of the generation who came of age in the Great Depression and World War II rejected the values and mores of their parents to an extent far greater than the expected generation imperative. They snubbed materialism and consumerism, voluntarily opting poverty over comfort. They embraced a new music, new and outlandish hairstyles and clothing, relaxed sexual practices aided and abetted by advances in oral contraception, and drugs, both old and new.

The rejection and defiance of the young earned them the scorn and derision of mainstream society. They became easy targets for conservative politicians and were the beneficiaries of fairly regular attention from law enforcement. The ever-present threat of conscription and deployment to Vietnam was an added factor that contributed to the sense of oppression felt by the young.

The oppressed status of the members of the 1960s counterculture was unique in that it was self-acquired, was acquired after childhood, and could be just as easily abandoned as it was acquired. Except for those who became permanent casualties of drug use or a very few dedicated souls who persevered into middle age with their counterculture values and lifestyles, the counterculture of the 1960s was, in the end, a temporary station on the road for most.

Because the 1960s counterculture was a cultural phenomenon that swept the young up in their teens or twenties, there was no indigenous language of the oppressed and the young were forced to borrow or invent. As illogical as it might seem for white middle-class youth to adopt the language of the black ghetto, the ghetto represented oppression and its language represented the most compelling example of the language of the oppressed, and so large blocks of the counterculture language were imported wholesale from the African-American vernacular. Most of the language newly coined by the counterculture dealt with drugs, especially the new-to-the-street drug LSD. Finally, the 1960s counterculture was inclusive to a fault, and so simple words such as "thing" and "it" and "like" and "shit" and "together" and "beautiful" became important building blocks of the language, making it possible for the uninitiated to understand and be understood without much difficulty.

The entire counterculture was an intentional culture, and for this reason the language of the counterculture was not as focused on constructing a positive collective identity as is the language of other oppressed groups. The public called the new counterculture young **hippies**, a word that was fittingly unoriginal, borrowed from the term used to describe jazz enthusiasts of the 1950s. In general, the young did not call themselves hippies, opting instead to affirm their identity by calling themselves **freaks** or **heads**. The term **freak** is fully discussed in Chapter Six as a hate word turned positive. **Head** (1911) was not an original coinage, and had been around for almost sixty years when taken up by the new counterculture. The original meaning and strong suggestion is of a drug user, but even the rare non-drug-using counterculturist would be self-described as a **head**.

※ ※ ※

A night club on the Sunset Strip called The Trip was obviously a gathering place for **heads**.
　　—Lawrence Schiller in Richard Alpert and
　　　Sidney Cohen: *LSD* (1966) 8

Trouble is, **heads** don't take care of themselves.
> —Nicholas Von Hoffman: *We Are The People Our Parents Warned Us Against* (1967) 211

A few thousand of the absolutely most together and peaceful and loving and beautiful **heads** in the world are gathered in a grand tribal new beginning.
> —*East Village Other* (August 28, 1969)

So, if **heads** on the land are responsible to their environment and its inhabitants (and not all of them are), then potential opponents at the barricades may have second thoughts.
> —*The Last Supplement to the Whole Earth Catalog* (1971) 90

In the counter-narrative of the oppressed, inversion is seen in role models and language. With the language of the counterculture of the 1960s, bad is good and vice versa. **Freak**, normally bad, is good, while **square** and **straight**, normally good, are bad. **Square** is directly scrounged from the African-American vernacular, but **straight** was new, referring as an adjective (1960) or noun (1967) to a conventional, conforming, mainstream person.

⚟ ⚟ ⚟

Of course they were all **straight**. They weren't into any crime or stuff like that, as far as I know.
> —Claude Brown: *Manchild in the Promised Land* (1965) 185

I walked toward them & thru them—was almost busted—but my guardian angel (temporarily acquired) looked **straight** enough to get us through.
> —*The San Francisco Oracle* (1965)

There were a few **straights** but they looked very uptight
and out of place.
—*Berkeley Barb* (January 20, 1967) 1

Straights shit in their pants when they hear the yippies
repeat the most crucial political issue in Amerika today:
pay toilets.
—Jerry Rubin: *Do It!* (1970) 86

Yes, some of us do have **straight** jobs and others devote
most of their time to the movement.
—*The Last Supplement to the Whole Earth Catalog*
(March 1971) 15

Just as mainstream society scorned the counterculture, the counterculture scorned mainstream society and its language reflected this scorn.
On loan from black slang and in constant use were **the man** and **pig**,
while **the Establishment** (1955) was borrowed from the 1950s.

❊ ❊ ❊

Here is a list of names, those who constitute the real
crème de la crème of Los Angeles power and influence.
This is "**the establishment**."
—*Los Angeles Free Press* (October 22, 1964) 2

If we do our job well, we hope even to nettle that
amorphous but thickhided **establishment** that so often
nettles us.
—*The Berkeley Barb* (August 31, 1965) 4

They may have washed their hands of **the
Establishment**, but in many ways that is quite
understandable.
—*Life Magazine* (March 31, 1967) 15

My note was "Fuck **the Establishment**." I wonder if
they used it.
    —*The Realist* (1968) 16

His main trip is anti-**Establishment**, and we can beat
him like a gong on that one.
    —Hunter S. Thompson: *Songs of the Doomed*
    (1971) 35

To show their scorn for mainstream values, the counterculture young
at times resorted to spelling "America" as **Amerika** (1969), denoting fascism by the Germanic "k."

Berkeley Cop Conspiracy: All-**Amerikan** Fascism
    —*The Berkeley Barb* (August 2–September 4,
    1969) 11

I am a child of **Amerika**. If I'm ever sent to Death Row
for my revolutionary "crimes," I'll order as my last meal:
a hamburger, French fries, and a Coke.
    —Jerry Rubin: *Do It!* (1970) 12

These black singers and magic music-makers were the
real "freedom riders" of **Amerika**.
    —John Sinclair: *Guitar Army* (1972) 12

Generally missing from the lexicon of the counterculture is a vocabulary
demonstrating disdain for those among the counterculture who side with
the oppressor, for the simple reason that the voluntary nature of the counterculture, those who sided with the oppressor simply returned to their
middle-class life, abandoning the counterculture. The only middle ground
between the counterculture and the dominant society was the recreational,
occasional visitor, referred to with derision as a **plastic hippie** (1967).

▓▓ ▓▓ ▓▓

PLASTIC HIPPIE—part-time hippie.
    —Joe David Brown: *The Hippies* (1967) 219

You began to hear stories out of the Haight saying the
"real" hippies were taking flight to rural communities
and that ersatz **plastic hippies** and teeni-boppers had
taken over.
> —Nicholas Von Hoffman: *We Are The People Our
> Parents Warned Us Against* (1967) 119

The bulk of these "Meth" or "speed freaks" come from
the lower "**plastic hippie**" class.
> —Lewis Yablonsky: *The Hippie Trip* (1968) 36

The final characteristic of the counterculture language that fits the profile of slang as resistance is its deliberate vulgarity. The music of the counterculture flaunted profanity, from Country Joe McDonald (who changed the "FISH" crowd cheer to a "FUCK" crowd cheer when performing "Fixin' To Die Rag") to the Jefferson Starship ("In order to survive, we cheat, lie, forge, fuck, hide, and deal") to the MC Five ("Kick out the jams, motherfuckers"). Likewise the language of the young, who spoke as if they were trying to prove to all just how very alienated/oppressed/natural they were in every sentence. Sexual liberation was an orthodoxy of the counterculture, and the young flaunted their sexuality and sexual mores as badges of honor. Not surprisingly, coarse sexual slang pervaded the language of the counterculture. Both the conduct and language were intentionally shocking, fitting the pattern of slang as resistance.

Workers of the World

A Marxist point of view is not necessary to perceive the divide between those who control the workplace and those who are controlled in the workplace. Although the oppression of contemporary domestic American capitalism may be mild by historical standards, the gulf between boss and worker is real. Johnny Paycheck's 1977 recording of "Take This Job and Shove It" would not have achieved its immense national popularity had it not struck a deep us-and-them nerve in the American worker. The well-documented language of railroad workers, loggers, and oil field workers displays the creative use of slang as everyday resistance to workplace authority, domination, and oppression.

Through their vernacular, workers proclaim their pride in their work and their role in society. The railroader will praise another worker as an **artist** or an **old hand**. An oil field worker can help no higher praise on a fellow worker than to say that he will **make a hand** or is a **real pipe hand**. A **hard face** is the ultimate praise from a logger for another logger.

The word that epitomizes the linguistic pride of workers is **boomer**, meaning an itinerant worker. The word was originally coined to describe railroad workers who were blackballed after participating in the railway strikes of the late nineteenth century.

❄ ❄ ❄

The stories of these raids will illustrate the hardships of **boomer** life.
—*The Chautauquan* (1889) 535

I wish to . . . throw some light on why so many railroad men become **boomers.**
—*Brotherhood of Locomotive Firemen and Engineers Magazine* (March 1911) 389

The term has come to be applied to workers in many industries, with the verb **to boom** used to mean to travel from job to job. Railroad workers use **boomer** as well as **Pocatello yardmaster** for itinerant workers, while loggers use **boomer** and **tramp logger**. Construction linemen use **boomer** regularly to this day, although they also use **tramp** as both noun and verb. In fact, the Local Union Director published by the International Brotherhood of Electrical Workers is universally known by linemen and wiremen as "The Tramp Guide."

The slang of workers is replete with terms for bosses, from the first-line foreman to the capitalist who owns the company. The terms range from jocular to deprecatory, with stops between, all of which place the power of naming in the worker with less power than the person being named. Ramon Adams collected a number of terms for bosses from the railroad in *The Language of the Railroader* (1977), including **bear cat** (an unpopular foreman), **brass collar**, **brass hat**, **general** (a yardmaster), the lighthearted **old man** heard in the military and prisons, **silk hat**, and **super**. To this list the *American Thesaurus of Slang* adds **bull goose** (a yardmaster), **dinger** (a yardmaster), **grandpa** (a general manager), **jig-gerooski** (a yardmaster), **main pin, master mind** (a yardmaster), **slave driver** (a yardmaster), and **tin hat** (a general manager).

In the oil fields, boss terms include **big shot, the Man, old man, real shot** ("Pipeline Diction" by Orlan Savey in *Texas Folk and Folklore*, 1954, by Mody Boatright et al., 323), **pressure, kingfish, headknocker** ("Oil Patch Talk" by James Winfrey in Boatright et al., 329), and **pusher** ("Pipeline Diction" by Orlan Sawey in *Backwoods to Border* [1943] edited by Mody Boatright et al., 201). Additional terms from the oil fields found in the *American Thesaurus of Slang* are **farm boss** and **nipple chaser** (the drilling superintendent).

The lexicon of loggers as recorded by McCulloch includes **big tyee, big wheel, boss logger, bull of the woods, camp push** (a logging camp foreman), **cheater** (a timekeeper), **head push** (a superintendent), **king snipe, log getter, log pusher, muzzler, old man, push, ramrod**, and **straw boss** (a temporary foreman). An overly frugal employer is a **belly robber**, and in a camp run by him the **holes in the doughnuts are too big**. An employment agent is a **man shark** and a dishonest scaler who measures the scale of logs is said to be **handy with the thumb**. A foreman who pushes loggers to work hard and fast is said to **bull 'em through, rawhide** (Sorden and Vallier, 167), or **ramrod** (McCulloch, 146). **Big bull, big savage, brass nuts, bully, gaffer, slave pusher**, and **uncle** are additional terms found in the *American Thesaurus of Slang*.

The termination of employment is a central point in a worker's life, and the vernacular of workers is present and willing with words and phrases, controlling linguistically the ultimate decision in employment. From the oil fields comes the term **drag up** for quitting a job:

⁑ ⁑ ⁑

"I'm ready to **drag up** (quit). I've got money in the bank and cattle out west."
> —James Winfrey: "Oil Patch Talk" in *Texas Folk and Folklore* (1954) edited by Mody Boatright et al., 327

In *Texas Crude* (1984), Ken Weaver asserts that the term "Derives from the habit of welders carefully and neatly pulling their lines up to the truck and coiling them up on their reels." (94). A logger who is quitting his job will **ask for his time** when he quits a job (McCulloch, 4) or **throw in** (*Ibid,* 193), asking the foreman to **make her out** or **write me up** (Sorden and Vallier, 132). If fired, the logger is given **a dose of hike** (*Ibid,* 1), told to **roll his blanket** (*Ibid,* 152), and will **tie a can on** (*Ibid,* 193).

The richest vein in the mine of worker vernacular comes in the language used to describe workers who betray their class and who side with employers, especially during strikes. Four key words express the disdain that workers feel for strikebreakers and company sycophants— **scab** (1777), **rat** (1824), **scissor-bill** (1913), and **fink** (1926).

The big enchilada of the scorn words is the oldest, **scab**, which unionists have used for more than 200 years to describe a worker who is disloyal to his union and fellow workers, most especially a worker who is willing to break a strike. Damon Runyon waxed poetic about strikers, penning "The Strikebreakers' Song" in 1911:

:: :: ::

> An', followin' on, they talked it in the field; the bible it
> puts that plain,
> An' Abel the Union Man, no doubt, he joshed at the
> work o' Cain—
> With many a stingin' word, perhaps, a' many a verbal
> jab,
> An' when Cain started to work ag'in, his brother he
> called him "**Scab!**"
> —Damon Runyon: *The Tents of Trouble* (1911) 25

The most famous use of the word **scab** is by someone who didn't write what he is purported to have written—Jack London. Within the American labor movement, there is no prose that is more famous than "The Definition of a Scab" attributed to Jack London. It begins with "After God finished the rattlesnake, the toad, the vampire, He had some awful substance left with which he made a scab. A scab is a two-legged animal with a cork-screw soul, a water-logged brain, a combination backbone of jelly and glue."

It is a fine piece of rhetorical hyperbole, but—the thing is—it does not appear in London's published work. The style of the "definition" is demotic, and students of London note that London's prose was not demotic. They further point to passages in the "definition" that bear remarkable resemblance to previously published definitions vilifying knockers, stool pigeons, and scandal-mongers.

So, then, the famous Jack London's Definition of a Scab, beloved by decades of labor leaders, is a powerful little piece of writing but is almost certainly not Jack London's. This fact will not stop it from being called Jack London's Definition, and because the diatribe and the word are so powerful, the definition will no doubt live on. The term **scab** certainly does:

▓ ▓ ▓

She issued an injunction that banned baseball's management from establishing its own work rules in the absence of a new collective bargaining agreement, and clearly blocked any attempt that management would have made at the time to try to play the '95 season with replacement players, which means **scabs.**
> —Mike Lupica: *Daily News (New York)* (May 27, 2009) 59

The union hiring halls that once existed in the cities have been replaced by "Centros de Jornaleros," subsidized by taxpayers money, where **scab** contractors hire scab labor and nobody pays taxes.
> —Letter to Editor, *Contra Costa (California) Times* (July 25, 2009)

In spring training of 1995 he decided to pitch in spring training games manned by replacement players, which led to him being labeled a replacement player himself, branded a "**scab.**"
> —"Toledoan Realized a Dream," *Toledo Blade* (August 9, 2009) C2

The thoroughly modern **rat** is surprisingly old, having referred to a strike-breaker or non-union worker for almost 200 years. Construction unions are fond of the **rat** image, going so far as to drive a huge inflatable gray rubber rat with red eyes to picket lines protesting substandard wages and working conditions.

Rat remains a popular term as it closes in on its 200th birthday, probably because it requires no guessing as to the sentiment behind it.

> A January union newsletter identifies non-members who "seem to have forgotten who their brothers and sisters are." It reads: "When called upon to do a **RAT** (scab) a favor, remember your UNION brothers are paying monthly dues."
> —Mike Berry: "Stress, Tempers Simmer at Seminole Fire Stations," *Orlando Sentinel* (February 17, 1992) B1

> Chet Karnas stood stone-faced at the front of Hotel St. Francis on Thursday morning as men paraded in an oval just a few feet away, loudly calling him and his company, Lone Sun Builders, **rats.**
> —Phil Parker: "Contractor Counters Union Protestors," *Albuquerque Journal* (June 6, 2009) C5

Rat may become a victim of its own success. As unions emphasize their ability to collaborate with employers, fighting words such as **rat** may be left behind.

⁜ ⁜ ⁜

> "We all work together on many projects, union or nonunion. I just find it insulting to call our nonunion counterparts **rats** or scabs."
> —Matt Glynn: "Building Trades Exterminate Their Rat," *Buffalo News* (August 24, 2009)

Emmett Murray in *The Lexicon of Labor* (1998) states that **scissorbill** was "a derogatory term dating from 1871 for law-abiding citizens who settled in Western frontier towns who were determined to clean up the 'rowdy' elements." (161). During the union organizing drives of the Industrial Workers of the World—the Wobblies—in the first decade of the twentieth century, the term came to deride workers who did not align themselves with fellow members of the working class. The earliest citation found to date in this sense is in the Oxford English Dictionary from the May 1, 1913, edition of an IWW newspaper in Spokane, Washington.

The most famous use of the term is in the song "Scissor Bill" by IWW organizer and labor icon Joe Hill, deriding his lack of class consciousness:

> Don't try to talk your union dope to **Scissor Bill**,
> He says he never organized and never will.
> He always will be satisfied until he's dead,
> With coffee and a doughnut and a lousy old bed.

The explicit discussion of class consciousness has all but disappeared from discourse within the American labor movement, and so has use of the word **scissor-bill**. Ramon Adams recorded it in *The Language of the Railroader* (133) as an uncomplimentary term for a new worker, and older power linemen still recognize the term, applying it to various people, most commonly electrical engineers. Gone but not quite forgotten, **scissor-bill** was a great gesture of resistance.

Last on the scene was **fink**, which had been used since 1903 as a general term of derision for an informer or anyone who betrayed group interests. The January 1926 edition of *American Mercury* claims that the term as applied to a strikebreaker dates from the 1891 Homestead strike and that it is a corruption of a "Pink," an abbreviation of "Pinkerton," the strike-breaking agency at Homestead.

Fink reached its zenith as a worker word of derision during the 1934 general strike in San Francisco, when dock and maritime workers named their membership books in company unions **fink books**. To go with the linguistic resistance, union workers publicly burned their **fink books** as a declaration of independence from their employers.

❖ ❖ ❖

Later, I heard the truth from another **fink** (strike-breaker).
　　　　—May Churchill Sharpe: *Chicago May* (1929) 272

SENATOR LA FOLLETTE. What is a **fink**?

MR. LAWSON. A strikebreaker.

> —"Violations of Free Speech and Rights of
> Labor," Hearings Before Senate Committee
> on Education and Labor (1936) 182

Detroit's "**fink** market" was located at Grand Circus
Park at Woodward Avenue, near the Statler Hotel.

> —Stephen Norwood: *Strikebreaking and
> Intimidation* (2002) 9

Worker use faded through the 1940s and 1950s and the specific sense of "strikebreaker" has been all but lost today.

The big four scorn words dominate but do not quite monopolize the market. The railroader used the term **lone wolf** or simply **wolf** for the non-union worker (Adams, 95). Both the logger and the oil field worker used **graper** or **grape picker** to describe someone who curries favor with his supervisor (McCulloch, 73; Winfrey, 328).

Jewish Immigrants

Between 1890 and 1910, approximately 1.5 million Eastern European Ashkenazic Jews immigrated to the United States. Three-quarters of them were literate, and most were multi-lingual, speaking at least one native language—Russian, Polish, Lithuanian, Hungarian, Bohemian, Rumanian—as well as the *linga franca*, the transactional language of Yiddish. The older members of the first generation of immigrants were not likely to learn more than 100 words of English. By the third generation, the grandchildren of immigrants were usually English-speakers, with their ethnic language and Yiddish used as private languages in the home (Teresa Labov: "English Acquisition by Immigrants to the United States at the Beginning of the Twentieth Century" in *American Speech,* Volume 73: 368–98, Winter 1998.) Yiddish served one other purpose, and that was to resist oppression.

The oppression suffered by Jewish immigrants and their progeny was two-pronged. On the one hand, they were despised as immigrants. Never mind Emma Lazarus' words on the Statue of Liberty, never mind the comfort promised to "your tired, your poor, your huddled masses yearning to breathe free." Then, as now, immigrants were not seen by all as the brave pioneers carrying on an American tradition that they are, but as others to be feared, distrusted, despised, scapegoated, and deported.

The second prong of oppression was anti-Semitism, both in the form of linguistic dehumanization and actual suppression and discrimination. Here as elsewhere, Jews have been singled out for harsh, even ruthless treatment. Overt anti-Semitism may not be tolerated in public discourse today, but until recently it was legally recognized in restrictive covenants, country club membership rules, and academic admission policies.

To combat oppression and the language of oppression, Jews have resorted to their old friend, the *linga franca* of Yiddish. Just as their first-generation immigrant ancestors mastered 100 words of English, Jews of the last decades have mastered fewer than 100 words of Yiddish, many of which have helped them define their Jewish identity and otherwise resist oppression. Yiddish is hard-wired for contempt, aspersion, sarcasm, and astringent derision. It has served its speakers well in resisting oppression.

Jewish immigrants used several Yiddish words or phrases to describe their immigrant experience, thereby exerting linguistic control over a reality over which they had very little control. **Greenhorn** had been used since 1753 to describe either a rustic from the countryside in the city or a freshly arrived immigrant; Jewish immigrants, who heard the word often, modified it to the Yiddish-sounding **greeneh** or **greener**.

❊ ❊ ❊

> The **greener** ran down the slip at the Staten Island ferry and flung himself into space, across the patch of water, landing on the boat with a terrific crash. He picked himself up, breathing hard, dusting off his trousers. "I made it!" "So what was your hurry," asked a passenger. "We're coming *in*."
> —Leo Rosten: *Hooray for Yiddish* (1982) 145

The wonder experienced in the new world was captured in the exclamation **America gonef!** (1971). The literal translation is "America the thief!", but it is not intended literally, only to express awe at the marvels, good and bad, of America.

⁙ ⁙ ⁙

> My mother, who was not financially illiterate, was
> soon calling America "**America Gonef**" (America the
> thief).
> —Harry Roskolenko: *The Time That Was Then*
> (1971)

> Its distant rhythms seemed far less turbulent than those
> of this thief America, or **America gonef**, as they so
> often called their new place of residence
> —Sherwin B. Nuland: *Lost in America* (2003) 27

Neither **greener** nor **America gonef!** survive in the contemporary vernacular, but they served their purpose for the first generation of immigrants.

The mere use of Yiddish demonstrated a cultural pride, and within the Yiddish were words that themselves expressed pride or helped establish identity. **Landsman** (1968) is largely forgotten, but it was used by the first wave of immigrants to refer to someone who hails from the same European hometown.

⁙ ⁙ ⁙

> "Why should you lose money on me, just because we
> happen to come from the same place? You are my
> *landsman* no less than I yours."
> —Leo Rosten: *The Joys of Yiddish* (1968) 204

Two Yiddish words which have survived over the generations as landmarks of identity are **chutzpah** (1892) and **mensch** (1953). **Chutzpah** is an especially Jewish combination of fortitude, courage, and gall—a perfect combination to stand up to oppression.

⚏ ⚏ ⚏

"You know, someone had the **chutzpah** to ask me the
other day—they said, "Tell me something, Doctor of
Law, is there a God or not?"
>—Lenny Bruce: *How to Talk Dirty and Influence
>People* (1967) 184

The gall, the **chutzpah**, her bringing a girlfriend along.
>—Sal Yurick: *The Bag* (1968) 214

I'm talking about Vice President Dick Cheney. For
him to be questioning Sen. John Kerry's ability and/or
willingness to protect this nation takes, well, **chutzpah**.
>—*Oakland Tribune* (May 2, 2004)

Mensch is a word of highest praise, used for someone who is upstanding, honorable, dependable, and decent. The admiration that comes with the word is unrelated to wealth, success, or intelligence.

⚏ ⚏ ⚏

You could be a real **mensch**. You've got it in you. But
you're effing it up with all this egotistical shit.
>—Saul Bellow: *Herzog* (1964) 61

I had been a good sailor with a sterling record of
consistent performance, but I wasn't a **mensch**.
>—Lenny Bruce: *How to Talk Dirty and Influence
>People* (1967) 21

A linguistic device first used by Jewish immigrants and later by subsequent generations is the **shm-** (1929) construction, converting by reduplication English words into Yiddish-sounding words. The construction probably began with **fancy-shmancy** in New York by Lower East Side Jews, but endless variations have followed.

⁜ ⁜ ⁜

Disguise, schmuisguise. So you wear a gold earring?
That's a disguise too?
—Bernard Wolfe: *The Late Risers* (1954) 218

"Fancy-schmancy" was all she said to me on the phone.
—Phillip Roth: *Goodbye, Columbus* (1959) 14

"Happy-shmappy, she makes other people miserable!"
—Leo Rosten: *The Joys of Yinglish* (1989) 175

As do other oppressed people, Jews have a specialized vocabulary for
their oppressors, including **goy** (1841) for a gentile (**goyish** as an adjective, and **goyim** as the plural noun) and **shiksa** (for a gentile woman).
Either term can be used neutrally, but it can also be used with varying
degrees of venom and attitude.

⁜ ⁜ ⁜

He worships me because I'm a **goy**.
—Mary McCarthy: *The Group* (1963) 334

I like to talk Yiddish in front of him, especially if there
are **goy** cops in hearing distance.
—Abbie Hoffman: *Revolution for the Hell of It*
(1968) 18

He drank—of course, not whiskey like a **goy**, but
mineral oil and milk of magnesia.
—Phillip Roth: *Portnoy's Complaint* (1969) 3

All Drake's Cakes are **goyish**. Pumpernickel is Jewish.
—Lenny Bruce: *The Essential Lenny Bruce* (1975) 56

The fault lay with them, because they had never
approved Lee-Simon's marrying a **shiksa**—and a fair-
haired one at that.
—Clancy Sigal: *Going Away* (1961) 375

"That is a **shiksa**, there's a pink-nippled lady; that's one thing about the goyim."
—Lenny Bruce: *How to Talk Dirty and Influence People* (1967) 142

Moving beyond the Jewish/not-Jewish divide, Yiddish gave Jewish immigrants and their descendants a rich collection of disparaging terms for their oppressors and other brutes, including **alter kocker** (1968) for a grouchy old man, **farshtinkener** (1982) for disgusting, **gonif** (1839) for a thug, **momzer** (1947) for a bastard, **putz** (1952) for a jerk, **schmo** (1943) for a hapless jerk, **schmuck** (1892) for a jerk, and **schnook** (1948) for a pathetic jerk.

⚌ ⚌ ⚌

His lawyer, Jesse Vogel, one of Mason's entourage of **alter cocker** flunkies, is propositioning blondes.
—Josh Friedman: *When Sex Was Dirty* (2005) 9

"David Douglas Kleinn, the 'Douglas' a dead giveaway, you are not of my kindred blood, you **farshtinkener** Dutch fuck."
—James Ellroy: *White Jazz* (1992)

Then New York with Jimmy Walker—a heavy **gonif**, a master **gonif**, man.
—Lenny Bruce: *The Essential Lenny Bruce* (1975) 57

"A real **momzer**—you know what I mean?" Rosen nodded, she was calling Adams a bastard.
—Ronald Levitsky: *The Truth That Kills* (1994) 260

"A real **putz**. A major **putz**."
—Nicholas Von Hoffman: *Citizen Cohn* (1988) 407

The big brother. The big **schmoe**.
—George Johnson: *Ocean's Eleven* (1960) 81

I thought in my arrogance and heartbreak—discarded,
unread, considered junk-mail by this **schmuck**, this
moron, this Philistine father of mine!
　　　　—Phillip Roth: *Portnoy's Complaint* (1969) 8

He thinks anything peculiar or unpleasant will just go
away if he turns on the radio and some little **schnook**
starts singing.
　　　　—J. D. Salinger: *Franny and Zooey* (1961) 82

Finally, when self-identity, ethnic pride, and scorn for the oppressor
don't do the trick, the Yiddish-speaking immigrant invoked a linguistic
talisman to ward off evil—**kine-ahora** (1968).

▓ ▓ ▓

Still trying to block the evil eye: **kineahora**, please
don't crash the plane.
　　　　—Jodi Varon: *Drawing to an Inside Straight* (2006) 38

Mexican Americans

Just as Jewish and Irish and Italian and Scandinavian and German
and Chinese immigrants were scorned in earlier decades of the twentieth century, by the 1960s Mexican Americans moved into the dubi-
ous honor of being the most despised immigrant group. Anti-immigrant
groups today target Mexican Americans and other Latin American immigrants as freeloaders and worse, oblivious it seems to the reality that
like all immigrant groups, the Mexican and Latin American immigrants
bring with them a work ethic and capitalistic goals that far outshine
most of their domestic competitors in the labor market.

Especially in the southwest, Mexican Americans have been the victims of harsh oppression. Like other immigrant groups, the first generation of immigrant Mexicans remained relatively monolingual, with each
subsequent generation speaking more English and less Spanish. Mexican
Americans in the Southwest, even those whose families have been in
the United States for several generations, are likely to pepper their primarily English-language conversations with corrupted border Spanish.
Merely speaking Spanish, like merely speaking any mother tongue, is a

gesture of resistance. Within the vocabulary of today's Mexican Americans are several terms that strongly suggest resistance to oppression.

La raza (1927) is a term that is crucial in the linguistic construction of a positive identity for Mexican Americans. Literally "the race," **la raza** connotes much more and much less, a pride in an identity that is not confined by nationality, color, or race, with none of the nasty trappings of "master race," pride usually without any notion of supremacy.

⬛ ⬛ ⬛

Viva **la Raza!** became the slogan in San Antonio and Laredo, Texas. These words became slogans motivating men to action.
—Jose Angel Gutierrez: *La Raza and Revolution* (1972) 45

"That's why today we oppose some of this **La Raza** business so much. We know what it does. When **La Raza** means or implies racism, we don't support it."
—Jacques Levy: *Cesar Chavez* (1975) 123

La raza is often first associated with the Raza Unida Party, a third party organized on ethnic lines in early 1970 in Crystal City, Texas, by Jose Angel Gutierrez and Mario Compean. A slightly earlier political cause, "*Los Siete de la Raza*" gave the term publicity. It was the label attached to seven San Francisco youth, all Central Americans and none Mexican, who were accused, tried, and acquitted of murdering a San Francisco police officer in 1969.

Resisting the dominant culture's names for places, some Mexican Americans refer to the southwestern United States as **Aztlan** and most refer to their neighborhoods as the **barrio** (1939).

Aztlan originally referred to the legendary pre-Columbian home of the Nahua peoples (Aztec is nothing more than Nahuati for "people from Aztlan.") Mexican-American activists in the late 1960s picked up the term to refer to the portion of the Southwest United States annexed by the result of the Mexican American War. It is the ultimate in linguistic resistance—you are living in our land, not the other way around.

⠿ ⠿ ⠿

Aztlan belongs to those who plant the seeds, water
the fields, and gather the crops, and not to foreign
Europeans.
—Jack Forbes: *Aztecas del Norte* (1973) 174

We are a Nation. We are a union of free pueblos. We
are **Aztlan**.
—Francisco Rosales: *Chicano!* (1997) 181

Barrio is literally a Mexican ghetto, usually in a small town, but the
word projects a pride and sense of home, just as Jewish immigrants used
shtetl instead of "ghetto." The oppressor may see the area of town as
a ghetto, but to Mexican Americans it is a safe, supportive place, the
barrio.

⠿ ⠿ ⠿

Facing this alien new world, often separated from
friends and family, it is only natural that the new
Chicano arrival looks for a home in the **barrio**.
—Elizabeth Martinez: *Viva la Raza!* (1974) 235

Chavez lived in a southeast San Jose, California, **barrio**,
a Spanish-speaking poor area of town. It was called Sal
Si Puedes.
—Brenda Haugen: *Cesar Chavez* (2008) 9

When it comes to self-identity, **Chicano** (1947) is as important a
term as any in the lexicon of the oppressed. The term was originally
at least susceptible to a derogatory connotation, but in the mid- to late
1960s Mexican-American activists such as Corky Gonzalez in his 1966
paradigm-shifting poem "Yo Soy Joaquin" embraced the term as one of
empowerment:

And in all the fertile farmlands,
the barren plains,

the mountain villages,
smoke-smeared cities,
we start to MOVE.
La raza!
Méjicano!
Español!
Latino!
Chicano!
Or whatever I call myself.

The good drove out the bad, and **Chicano** emerged as a term of pride, having shed its past derisive associations.

❈ ❈ ❈

No man personifies the **Chicanos'** bleak past, restless present and possible future in quite the manner of Cesar Chavez.
—*Time Magazine* (July 4, 1969) 17

Chicano is a beautiful word. Chicano describes a beautiful people. **Chicano** has a power of its own. **Chicano** is a unique confluence of histories, cultures, languages, and traditions.
—Armando Rendo: *Chicano Manifesto* (1971)

Carnal (1950) is another proud term for a close and reliable friend. It was originally a term used by pachucos, but it survived into the English-dominated conversation of later generations of Mexican-American youth.

❈ ❈ ❈

They automatically became members of La Eme, the so-called Mexican Mafia, and were now sworn **carnales**, the Hispanic term for homeboys.
—Seth Morgan: *Homeboy* (1990) 176

A **carnal** had to be prepared to fight at all times.
—Bill Valentine: *Gangs and Their Tattoos* (2000) 33

Similarly, **ese** (1950) is a term of address coined by pachucos and embraced by subsequent generations in virtually the same manner that African Americans would use **man** as a term of respectful address.

❊ ❊ ❊

"What'd you get into this morning, **ese**?"
—Malcolm Braly: *Felony Tank* (1961) 44

Shit, **ese**, I mean just one joint.
—Oscar Zeta Acosta: *The Revolt of the Cockroach People* (1973) 230

Cholo was originally (1851) used to describe a Mexican of mixed Indian and Spanish heritage, but in the midst of the social movements of the 1960s and 1970s was embraced by activists (1971) as another term for a Mexican-American youth.

❊ ❊ ❊

The language of East L.A. is a speedy sort of **cholo** mixture of Mexican Spanish and California English.
—Hunter S. Thompson: *Fear and Loathing in Las Vegas* (1971) 1971

He saw a group of **cholos** in their oversized white T-shirts and baggy pants making their way through the yard.
—Michael Connelly: *The Black Ice* (1993) 379

Anglo youths especially imitated the distinctive dress of Mexican-American "**cholos**" with their khaki pants and long-sleeved Pendleton shirts.
—George Lipsitz: *Time Passages* (2001) 139

Another term used to describe an American-born Mexican American is pocho (1944), which is especially heard in California.

⠿ ⠿ ⠿

"I am a **Pocho**," he said, "and we speak like this
because here in California we make Castillian words
out of English words."
  —Jose Antonio Villarreal: *Pocho* (1959) 165

"But at **pocho** talk my mother drew the line."
  —Frances Von Maltitiz: *Living and Learning in
  Two Languages* (1975) 31

The language spoken by the **cholo** or **pocho** is **calo** (1970), a combination of corrupted Spanish, corrupted English, and slang from each language.

⠿ ⠿ ⠿

The language spoken at home is pocho, **calo.**
  —Thomas Carter: *Mexican Americans in School*
  (1970) 92

Calo, slang sprung from the pachuco complex,
universally used among Chicano youth, and visible as
graffiti on barrio walls.
  —Armando Rendon: *Chicano Manifesto* (1971) 30

Of considerable importance is the Border or Chicano
Calo, an argot which developed as "Pachuco" in the El
Paso area.
  —Felix Rodriguez Gonzalez: *Spanish Loanwords
  in the English Language* (1996) 186

A final term of praise is vato loco, sometimes seen as bato loco. It first appeared in Spanish text in 1953, and in English text in 1965. The literal translation is "crazy guy," but the term implies more, it suggests a degree of resistance against the dominant culture.

:: :: ::

This label implies a permanency of behavior and a prediction: once a Mexican American becomes a **vato loco**, he will continue to perform those acts and engage in those activities which "fit" the label.
> —George B. Alvarez: *Semantic Dynamics of an Ethnic-Amerian Sub-Cultural Group* (1965) 4

"The **vato loco** has truly been at the forefront of the Chicano Revolution."
> —Stan Steiner: *La Raza* (1970) 119

Evolving through the **bato loco** (crazy guy) complex and pachuca cant, con safos came to signify defiance.
> —Armando Rendon: *Chicano Manifesto* (1971) 30

In the cities, only the lowriders, the **vatos locos**, are in tune with this.
> —Oscar Zeta Acosta: *The Revolt of the Cockroach People* (1973) 67

The language of oppression is replete with derogatory terms for Mexican Americans, and it is only natural that Mexican Americans have a few derisive terms of their own to describe their white Anglo-Saxon oppressors. **Gringo** (1849) is the best-known term but it is rarely used today by other than **gringo** speakers.

:: :: ::

I am a Chicano because from this revived and newly created personality I draw vitality and motivation more forceful and tangible than I ever did or could have from the **gringo** world.
> —Armando Rendo: *Chicano Manifesto* (1971) 201

Most Mexicans have become used to the "stupid **gringo**" who travels south to take a cut-rate vacation, drink cheap beer, and buy souvenirs.
>—Trevor Cralle: *The Surfin'ary* (2001) 242

The contemporary and modern term of choice is **gabacho** (1971), often said with a sneer and scorn.

❏ ❏ ❏

As is the case with stereotypes of Chicanos, Pitt's use of **Gabacho** stereotypes is problematic.
>—*El Grito* (1972) 22

Almost all of our respondents were more willing to use Anglo and **gabacho**, with most denying the use of gringo and a few adding "White."
>—Gerald Rosen: *Political Ideology and the Chicano Movement* (1975) 65

Did I ever tell you the fable of the trout and the **gabacho** baby? No?
>—John Nichols: *The Magic Journey* (1978) 474

Two other Spanish words are used in English conversation by Mexican Americans to describe their oppressors—**chota** for police, and **la migra** for the Immigration and Naturalization Service.

❏ ❏ ❏

It is sure that **la chota** will be back tomorrow with more men.
>—Carol Norquest: *Rio Grande Wetbacks* (1972) 124

La chota reigns supreme in the barrio; he relentlessly maintains his role of guardian of the gringo's world.
>—Armando Rendon: *Chicano Manifesto* (1971) 239

> **La migra** is the term conferred by Chicanos upon
> the Border Patrol, a racist-motivated branch of the
> Department of Justice.
> > —Armando Rendon: *Chicano Manifesto* (1971) 201

> This is **La Migra**—the US Immigration Service, the
> Border Patrol.
> > —Elizabeth Martinez: *Viva la Raza!* (1974) 326

As is the case with almost all oppressed groups, there is a special place in linguistic hell for members of the oppressed class who curry favor with their oppressors. With Mexican Americans, the term of choice is **Tio Taco** (1967), literally "Uncle Taco," an obvious evolution from the African-American term **Uncle Tom**.

※ ※ ※

> A Negro catering to whites is called a "Tom" (from
> "Uncle Tom," and equivalent to the Chicano term "**Tio
> Taco**" in Los Angeles).
> > —Carroll Reed: *Dialects of American English*
> > (1967) 76

> "It makes him impotent, a **Tio Taco**, an Uncle Tom. I
> was losing my cool," Gonzales says. "I was used by the
> Democratic Party."
> > —Stan Steiner: *La Raza* (1970) 383

> Al Espinosa, Delano's Mexican-American police
> captain, who had been severely ostracized by the union
> as a "sell-out" and a "**Tio Taco**," was particularly bitter
> about the strike.
> > —Jerry Brown: *The United Farm Workers Grape
> > Strike and Boycott* (1972) 231

The term **vendido** is heard in broader context, used as a nearly direct translation of "sell-out." Its most prominent use was probably in Jose Montoya's 1969 poem "El Vendido."

CHAPTER 6

Hate Words—Swords Into Plowshares

C entral to any oppression is a language of oppression, words that are used to dehumanize a segment of the population. In *The Language of Oppression* (1974), Haig Bosmajian studies the link between the segregation and separation of an oppressed people and the language used to dehumanize them. He observes that the language of anti-Semitism, of white racism, of Indian derision, of sexism, and of war all are "used to justify the unjustifiable, to make palatable the unpalatable, to make reasonable the unreasonable, to make decent the indecent." (9)

Psychologist Gordon Allport quantified oppression, using what has become known as Allport's Scale of Prejudice. There are five degrees in Allport's scale, starting with "antilocution" and ending with extermination. Allport uses "antilocution" to refer to hate speech or ethnophaulisms (ethnic slurs). To the oppressor, the negative images conjured up by speech often appears harmless, but its purpose is to pave the way for more harmful manifestations of prejudice.

One tactic of those who wish to resist oppression is to overtly rebel against linguistic suppression and to work directly to curtail use of ethnic slurs and other hate words. This is not the only tactic available, though. Another weapon in the slang arsenal of the oppressed is to seize the language of the oppressor and to use what had been derogatory as a positive, a linguistic beating of swords into plowshares and spears into pruning hooks. The use of what had been words of hate as words of pride is always controversial within the oppressed group, with the young and radical members of the group on the vanguard and the older, more conservative members reacting with caution if not outright opposition to any use at all of words of hate.

The philosophy behind the conversion of hate to pride is neatly explained in Kevin Smith's 1997 comedy movie *Chasing Amy*, which revolves around sexual identity. In this scene, the linguistic hijacking of hate words is explained by Alyssa, a lesbian comic-book writer played by Joey Lauren Adams:

> HOLDEN
>
> You're blowing this way out of proportion. We live in a more tolerant age now. You refer to yourself as a dyke. Hooper calls himself a faggot all the time . . .

> ALYSSA
>
> Yeah, but that's what's known as empowerment/disempowerment. I call myself a dyke so it's not too devastating when some throwback screams it at me as I'm leaving a bar at night.
>
> Same for Hooper—by calling himself a faggot, he steals the thunder away from the mouthy jerks of this world who'd like to beat him to it. But the difference between us having it and your friend saying it is miles wide. We say it to mask the pain—you say it for lack of a better expression at any given moment. No, Holden, we do not live in a more tolerant age. And if you think that's the case, then you've been in the suburbs way too long to be resuscitated.

This phenomenon has been touched upon in earlier discussions of **Chicano** in the Mexican-American community and **grunt** in the military, and is kin to the world upside down dynamic, where what they say is bad is good to us. It goes further though, than simple inversion, and evidences both a desire to de-stigmatize a world of hate and a desire to build a proud self-identity where scorn and derision had lived.

Lavender Menace

An early example of the conversion of a term of disparagement into a term of pride by an oppressed group is powerful—the embrace of the term **Lavender Menace** by lesbian activists within the broader women's movement in the early 1970s. In the nascent years of the women's movement, heterosexual feminists such as National Organization of Women president Betty Friedan worried that the participation of lesbians in feminist organizations would detract from the movement's chances of success. Accordingly, in 1969, Friedan removed the lesbian organization the Daughters of Bilitis as a sponsor of the First Congress to Unite Women.

In March 1970, radical feminist Susan Brownmiller wrote about the issue in the *New York Times Magazine*, quoting Friedan as having used the term "**lavender menace**" to describe the threat to the women's movement posed by lesbian activists. The reaction by lesbian activists was swift, creative, and humorous. At the Second Congress to Unite Women held on May 1, 1970, lesbians infiltrated the audience and as the event began, they hijacked it, wearing purple "**Lavender Menace**" T-shirts, diverting the program to an open-microphone discussion of the role of lesbians in the feminist movement.

From this point forward, **lavender menace** assumed a positive, if humorous, connotation. The term is rarely used any longer, but when it is, it is with humor, mocking those who fear lesbians and homosexuals, as in this opinion piece from the June 24, 2006, *Daily News Leader* from Stanton, Virginia: "Straight out of the starting gate, almost before the echo from the Speaker's gavel had died, Virginia passed a measure that could result in amending the state constitution so that we will all be protected from the **Lavender Menace.** To hear our brave legislators talk, you'd think that gays were tossing bouquets from the steps of every church in the Commonwealth. They're not, and gay marriage is already illegal in Virginia, but it was important that the first act of this General Assembly was to make gay marriage illegaller." One less sword, one more plowshare.

African American

As is fitting for the group whose oppression tops the charts, African Americans have endured chart-topping racial epithets for centuries, including the atom bomb of hate speech, **nigger**. It is at least one of the two most carefully avoided words in the English language, and perhaps the most—O.J. Simpson assistant prosecutor Christopher Darden labeled it "the dirtiest, filthiest, nastiest word in the English language" (*Los Angeles Times*, December 13, 1995, Page A16), despite the fact that Darden's witness Detective Mark Fuhrman had said that "all those niggers in L.A. City government . . . should be lined up against a wall and fucking shot" and that Ethiopians were "a bunch of dumb niggers that their own government won't even feed."

Over the years, the use of "**nigger**" has faded from social discourse. Despite the rapid decline in the term's use, there have been several relatively recent high-profile efforts to banish the word completely by activists whom Randall Kennedy, author of *Nigger: The Strange Career of a Troublesome Word*, calls eradicationists. For example, in 1998 NAACP President Kweisi Mfume threw the weight of his organization behind a threatened boycott of Merriam-Webster because of the dictionary's definition of the term. In 2006, Jesse Jackson urged a boycott of all entertainment media that used the word **nigger**, including Twain's *The Adventures of Huckleberry Finn*, Mel Brooks' *Blazing Saddles*, *Redd Foxx Uncensored*, and *Bicentennial Nigger* by Richard Pryor. Neither effort produced any perceptible effect on the market despite substantial media attention.

Another approach has been to defang **nigger** by freely using it. If the word is used extensively, the theory goes, its stigma will evaporate and its allure to the racist will fade. Lenny Bruce famously urged the president to go on television and announce "Tonight I'd like to introduce the niggers in my cabinet" (*Essential Lenny Bruce*, 11). Fast forward three decades and director and screenwriter Quentin Tarantino picked up the same thread: "I also feel that the word 'nigger' is one of the most volatile words in the English language and any time anyone gives a word that much power, I think everybody should be shouting it from the rooftops to take the power away."

Some African-American comedians have followed the "shout it from the rooftops" with glee. Redd Foxx was not shy about using the word **nigger** in his nightclub act on his "blue" "party" records. Dick Gregory didn't overuse the word, but he titled his 1964 autobiography *Nigger* and joked in the Preamble: "Dear Momma—Wherever you are, if ever you hear the word 'nigger' again, remember they are advertising my book."

He ends the book with a hope: "And now we're ready to change a system, a system where a white man can destroy a black man with a single word. **Nigger**. When we're through, Mama, there won't be any **niggers** any more."

Richard Pryor, as funny a man as ever lived, openly and notoriously used the word **nigger** in his act and albums, including Grammy-winning albums in 1974 "That Nigger's Crazy" (with tracks including "Nigger with a Seizure" and "Niggers vs. Police") and 1976 "Bicentennial Nigger" (including the monologue "Bicentennial Nigger"). Pryor, playing a job applicant, and Chevy Chase, playing a prospective employer, performed a sketch on *Saturday Night Live* in 1975 that was brilliant if unthinkable by today's standards, in which they swap racist insults. When Chase puts Pryor into check with the ultimate slur of **nigger**, Pryor reverses and puts Chase in checkmate with "dead honky." In 1979 Pryor visited Africa, and his use of the word **nigger** trailed off and disappeared. In his 1982 "Live on the Sunset Strip" album, he explained his epiphany: "When I was in Africa, this voice came to me and said, 'Richard, what do you see?' I said, 'I see all types of people.' The voice said, 'But do you see any **niggers**?' I said, 'No.' It said, 'Do you know why?' "Cause there aren't any.'"

Chris Rock has taken up the rooftops torch, and in fact, his routine "Black People vs. Niggers" on his 1996 HBO Special "Bring the Pain" launched him into stardom—"There's like a civil war going on with black people. And there's two sides: there's black people and there's niggers. The niggers have got to go." He expanded in his 1997 book *Rock This*: "Everytime black people want to have a good time, **niggers** mess it up. You can't do anything without some ignorant-ass **niggers** fucking it up."

It has been hip-hop artists more than anyone else who have taken the word **nigger** and tried to beat it into a plowshare, although they were not the first recording artists to take a run at the word. In 1970, the Last Poets released "Niggers are Scared of Revolution," a passionate tirade against complacency: "Niggers are scared of revolution / But niggers shouldn't be scared of revolution / Because revolution is nothing but change / And all niggers do is change."

The group NWA (Niggas With Attitude) pioneered the new bold, defiant, self-empowering use of **nigga**, a deliberate re-spelling that was intended to differentiate their term of empowerment from the term of hate. Their song "Niggaz 4 Life" is built around the refrain "Why do I call myself a '**nigga**'?" and is a powerful indictment of racism—"I call myself a **nigga** 'cause my skin won't whiten / I call myself a **nigga** 'cause the shit that I'm writing / Hypes me, hypes other mother fuckers around me / And that's the reason why they want to surround me / And ask me: why do I call myself a **nigga**— / Ain't none of their fuckin' business . . . You're a **nigga** 'til you die / If you're a poor **nigga**, then you're a poor **nigga** / If you're a rich **nigga**, you're a rich **nigga** / But you never stop being a **nigga**." Dr. Dre, A Tribe Called Quest, Jay-Z, Geto Boys, DMX, Cypress Hill, Ice-T, Ice Cube, Coolio, and other famous rappers all toss **nigga** around without a care.

African-American elders have not taken kindly to the use of **nigger** or **nigga** by fellow African Americans. In 1993, the Reverend Calvin Butts of Abyssinian Baptist Church in Harlem, launched a campaign, generally ignored, against the words "nigga," "bitch," and "ho" in rap lyrics, urging a return to the kinder and gentler "brother" and "sister." At about the same time, the National Black Family Empowerment Agenda issued a manifesto Renouncing and Denouncing the use of the "N" word, stating that use as term of empowerment is "psychological bondage" and that there is "no positive or productive meaning" of the word. In his 2007 book *Come On, People*, Bill Cosby rejected any difference between **nigger** and **nigga** and argued that any use of the word suggests self-hatred.

As the use of **nigger** as a term of hate has waned, the use of **nigga** as an affirmation of power has waxed. Correlation does not automatically translate to causation, and it cannot be said with any degree of certainty that the use of **nigga** with pride has done what Lenny Bruce thought it would to **nigger** as a term of hate. Today, it is a term that is probably used more commonly by African Americans than whites, but another decade will tell whether either term survives, either as language of oppression or as language of resistance.

Dyke and Queer

For much of its early life, **dyke** (1942) was used as a venomous term of disparagement for any "mannish" woman, assuming that she was a lesbian. There was nothing kind or even neutral about **dyke**—it spat derision.

To the oppressed, a hate word is just a sword waiting to be beat into a plowshare, and so it was with **dyke**. The walls began tumbling down on **dyke** at the 1976 San Francisco Gay Pride parade, when the lead unit in the parade was a contingent of women motorcycle riders who proudly called themselves **Dykes on Bikes**. The idea—and the name—caught on, and there are now **Dykes on Bikes** chapters throughout the United States, and the San Francisco chapter continues more than thirty years later to lead the San Francisco Gay Pride parade.

The hijacking of **dyke** has not been without controversy. Lesbians have criticized the use of a term with such historically negative connotations. **Dykes on Bikes** have countered, first on the ground that they are motorcyclists who reject middle-class norms and middle-class sensibilities about language, and secondly on the ground that by using the word **dyke** with pride it has become a self-referential term of empowerment. Just as **Dykes on Bikes** challenge cultural assumptions of what women can and cannot do, they challenge cultural assumptions about language.

A second, less expected, challenge to the term **Dykes on Bikes** came from the United States Patent and Trademark Office when **Dykes on Bikes** attempted to register their name as a trademark. In 2004, the Patent and Trademark Office rejected registration of the name on the ground that the term **dyke** was disparaging and objectionable to a group of people—lesbians. The absurdity of this position is worthy of Kafka, for it was the very women whom the Patent Office feared would be disparaged who sought to use the name. After a three-year battle, **Dykes on Bikes**™ prevailed and won trademark protection for its name.

Following in the tread marks of their sisters, a direct-action group called the Lesbian Avengers took up the **dyke** banner in the first-ever **Dyke March** in 1993. The National Gay and Lesbian Task Force had organized a national March on Washington for gay rights. The Lesbian Avengers announced a **Dyke March** the night before the main event. Up to 20,000 lesbians joined the march, banging **dyke** from spear to pruning hook. Once **dyke** was breached, there was no turning back. **Dyke marches** have been held throughout the United States, and continue in conjunction with larger gay pride parades, usually held on the night before.

While **dyke** took a militant turn, **queer** took an almost academic turn. It had long been used as a dismissive if not derogatory term, first as a noun (1894) and later as an adjective (1914). Beat writers used **queer** without hesitation in the early 1950s as a hip way of saying "homosexual," not necessarily derogatorily, but its derogatory overtones did not disappear:

⠿ ⠿ ⠿

> Then I remembered that was an illiberal thing to say, and argued that even if he was a **queer** they shouldn't hold it against him. They did.
> —Clancy Sigal: *Going Away* (1961) 150

American colleges initiated Gay and Lesbian Studies programs in the 1970s, with the term "Queer Studies" beginning in the mid-1980s. In a world dominated by political correctness and terms such as gay, lesbian, bisexual, transgender, transsexual, intersexual, asexual, autosexual, and gender normative heterosexuals, **queer** stands out as a brilliant example of the hijacking of a former term of derision. By the new millennium, **queer** was no longer an "illiberal thing to say," and popular television shows such as *Queer Eye* (2003) and *Queer as Folk* (2000–2005 in the U.S. after an earlier appearance in the U.K.) used **queer** in a hip, colloquial sense. While **queer** can still be used as a term of hate, it is probably used more commonly as a term of pride and self-identity.

Hippies and Freaks

When the counter-cultural movement of the 1960s that came to be known as hippies first started to develop, the mainstream did not know what to call these long-haired, oddly dressed, drug-taking young people. "Beatnik" served for a while, but at some point it became obvious that this was a new phenomenon that required a new name. **Hippy** had been used since at least 1953 to mean a follower of jazz and the jazz scene, and so rather than inventing a completely new word, **hippy** was given a new assignment, first appearing in a series of articles about the Haight-Ashbury neighborhood in San Francisco in the *San Francisco Examiner* in September 1965.

Whatever formal label polite society used to describe the flower children, the easiest label and one heard regularly as **freak** or hippie **freak**, derisive, derogatory terms suiting for the contempt felt by decent society for these new young rebels. Hippies didn't take this lightly, and quickly they began to use **freak** as a self-descriptive term of pride. The earliest known citation in this new, empowerment sense, is from *Avatar*, an underground newspaper in Boston from 1967. The term quickly became the preferred self-applied label for hippies.

≋ ≋ ≋

Freak referred . . . just to heads in costume. It wasn't a negative word.
> —Tom Wolfe: *The Electric Kool-Aid Acid Test*
> (1968) 10

Anyway, I was struck by the distance between me and those street **freaks**.
> —Hunter S. Thompson: *Songs of the Doomed*
> (February 16, 1969), 119

Your average acid-eating **freak** will be getting arrested for attempting to sit in the park under General Thomas's horse in Thomas Circle.
> —Raymond Mungo: *Famous Long Ago (1970) 29*

Freak: The accepted word for those who are hip.
> —*Screw* (October 12, 1970) 7

Political hippie/yippie Jerry Rubin went one step further, tweaking the spelling of **freak** just as he preferred the Germanic **Amerika** to America:

≋ ≋ ≋

The university became a fortress surrounded by our foreign culture, longhaired, dopesmoking, barefooted **freeks** who were using state-owned university property as a playground.
> —Jerry Rubin: *Do It!* (1970) 26

Freak was more than just a word used in passing. In their 1970 song "Almost Cut My Hair," Crosby, Stills and Nash celebrated long hair, with the singer defiantly confessing that while he almost cut his hair, he decided not to because he wanted to let his "**freak** flag" fly. When Hunter S. Thompson ran for Sheriff of Pitkin County, Colorado, in 1970, he did so as part of the **Freak** Power (sometimes spelled **Freek** Power) movement promoting a platform that favored decriminalization of drugs and anti-growth policies.

What distinguishes **freak** from other hate words (aside from the fact that a person described as a **freak** could in most instances return to an appearance and lifestyle that would render the label inapplicable) is the alacrity with which those who were derided as **freaks** began to refer to themselves proudly as **freaks**. Central to the hippie ethos was a sentiment expressed by the Jefferson Starship in Paul Kantner's 1969 song "We Can Be Together"—"Everything they say we are, we are / And we are very proud of ourselves."

CHAPTER 7

Open Resistance: Gloves Off, Slang Gone

W hen an oppressed group steps from the relative safety of small acts of everyday resistance and instead begins to engage in overt, public resistance, what of the slang that has served them so well as a gesture of resistance? When a tipping point is reached and the momentum for direct resistance to oppression has become unstoppable, what happens to the language of the oppressed? Sadly, the slang evaporates, giving way to serious, standard English, the stilted, heartless, soulless language of social activism.

It is not that the oppressed who openly resist oppression suddenly care what the oppressors think, it is that they care what a broader audience outside their immediate community thinks. Their desire to be taken seriously is understandable, and political rhetoric is therefore appropriated. An additional factor helps explain the collapse of slang when resistance becomes open—when direct action is taken, the lesser, indirect actions that the oppressed had used instead of direct action are no longer necessary. Why use slang to build pride when political action does the same? Why use slang to mock the oppressor when direct action is being taken to challenge the oppressor's power and domination? In this instance, language is a zero-sum game—no room for both rhetoric and slang in the same space.

African American

African-American slang is the most vibrant, lively, creative, and graphic in the slang universe, and so its annihilation in the language of African-American social activism is a bitter pill to swallow. Because the slang is so lively, its loss is most easily observed and most dearly missed.

Geneva Smitherman observed in *Talkin and Testifyin* (1977) that "Since the Civil War, and in the twentieth century especially, upward mobility for Black Americans has come to mean the eradication of black language (and black culture) and the adoption of the linguistic norms of the white middle class." (173). It is not surprising that the upwardly mobile assimilationists moved towards white linguistic norms, but it is not intuitively obvious why political activists would do the same. Yet, they do. In *A Study of the Non-Standard English of Negro and Puerto Rican Speakers in New York City* (1968), William Labov et al. examined the language of black activists and concluded:

> In the present period of rising self-consciousness among Negro people, and the assertion of pride in ethnic identity, it would seem that NNE [non-standard Negro English] would swiftly come to the fore as a political and social badge of honor. This has not been the case so far, however; northern Negro leaders of all social backgrounds are fundamentally SE [standard English] speakers, and their concessions to the vernacular are superficial and trivial from a linguistic point of view. (Volume II, 218–19).

Labov's conclusion is what one might expect from civil rights leaders with academic or religious backgrounds, but for activists coming from the streets the rejection of "non-standard Negro English" is puzzling. Can it be true? It can be true. Say it ain't so! Sorry, it's so.

There was no group of black activists with more street credentials and street credibility than the Black Panther Party. They came from the ghetto, they worked to better the lives of those who lived in the ghetto, and they spoke to those who lived in the ghetto, and so it would be logical that their concessions to the vernacular would be more than superficial or trivial. Yet, they were not. The language used by members of the

Black Panther Party was impenetrable, clichéd, Marxist rhetoric. The vocabulary was artificial and a stark contrast to the creative indigenous slang that had been abandoned. Two short examples from the *Black Panther*, the party's newspaper, quickly and richly illustrate this point:

❇ ❇ ❇

The governing body of the Black Panther Party, which is our Central Committee, has decided that in order to preserve democratic centralism and to destroy ultra-democracy within our ranks, that it is of absolute necessity to understand the decadence of ultra-democracy. First, it must be crystal clear that ultra-democracy damages the party organization and seeks to undermine the Party. We must also point out that the petty bourgeoisie's individualistic aversion to discipline is directly related.
—Virtual Murrell: "Panther Purge" *The Black Panther* (January 25, 1969) 17

The People shall smash the glutton roaches running this decadent society and, along with the directing of the Black Panther Party, halt these running dogs and gain true liberation for all.
—"Serving the People," *The Black Panther* (April 6, 1969) 14

There was some vestigial slang in the lexicon on the Black Panthers, most notably their extensive and exclusive use of **pig** instead of police. What little slang survived was used for emphasis and it stands out, leading the reader to wonder why it is still there and so much great slang is not.

H. Rap Brown of the Student Nonviolent Coordinating Committee got his nickname "Rap" in his youth because of his ability to use the vernacular. When he became political, he abandoned the vernacular with dazzling completeness. In his provocatively titled *Die Nigger Die!* (1969), Brown coined one of his most famous quotes, but wrote without slang:

> The question of violence has been cleared up. This country was born of violence. Violence is as American as cherry pie. Black people have always been violent, but our violence has always been directed toward each other. If nonviolence is to be practiced, then it should be practiced in our community and end there. Violence is a necessary part of revolutionary struggle. Nonviolence as it is advocated by negroes is merely a preparation for genocide (144).

Labov spotted things correctly. Rather than use the rich body of black slang as a "political and social badge of honor," black activists have steered clear of the vernacular, opting instead for a standard English, if not the hyper-standard rhetoric of Marxist ideology. Ironically, in so doing, these activists have accepted white linguistic norms as freely and entirely as have those who from the start sought to assimilate in white America and have embraced white culture, value, and language.

Prison

In the early 1970s, two forces converged to form the radical prison movement. First, in sync with the times, at least a small core of prisoners became politicized and radicalized, seeing their lives and imprisonment as part of a bigger picture. Secondly, predominantly white radicals in the free world began a search for prison revolutionary leaders. The radicals latched onto a quotation from Ho Chi Minh: "When the prison gates fly open, the real dragons will emerge." Ignoring the fact that Ho Chi Minh was referring to prisoners who were imprisoned for their political activities and ignoring the difficulties inherent in converting a criminal mentality to a revolutionary mentality, the radicals were fiercely devoted to any African-American or Mexican-American prisoner who talked the talk of revolution. The Soledad Brothers (three African-American prisoners charged with the 1970 murder of a guard), the San Quentin Six (six prisoners charged with murder during the events surrounding the killing of George Jackson at San Quentin prison), and the leaders of the Attica prison revolt several weeks after Jackson's killing all became passionate causes of the Left.

The radical prison movement was short-lived, but made up for its short lifespan with the intensity with which it lived. In the end, the criminal mentality prevailed over the revolutionary mentality, and crime, not Marx, returned as the central organizing principle in prison life. While alive, though, the prison movement, like other movements of the oppressed, turned its back on the rich and wide-ranging slang that had flourished as seeds of resistance in prisons, embracing instead the new lover—the jargon of social activism.

George Jackson was the leading example of the revolutionary prisoner, both inside prison and with radicals in the free world. Jackson was if nothing else brilliant, and he wrote prolifically. From his *Soledad Brother* (1970) come these two excerpts, demonstrating the nature of the language he used:

> Class struggle means the suppression of the opposing class, and suppression of the Amerikan General Staff, and The Corporate Elite. The moment this three-headed monster detects the danger contained in our ideas and ideals, he will react violently against us. Just the whisper of revolt excites in him a swift and terrible reflex, so swift we won't even know how we died (227).

> The Amerikan fascist used a thousand similar devises, delaying maneuvers, to prevent a people from questioning the validity of the principles upon which capitalism is founded, to turn the people against themselves, people against people, people against other groups of people (239).

Less than two months before he was killed, George Jackson gave an interview to Karen Wald, which was later published in *Cages of Steel*. In that interview, Jackson demonstrated the degree to which he had rejected the vernacular even in his spoken English:

> The principle contradiction between the oppressor and oppressed can be reduced to the fact that the only way the oppressor can maintain his position is by fostering, nurturing, building contempt for the oppressed. That thing gets out of hand after a while. It leads to excesses that we see and the excesses are growing within the totalitarian state here. The excesses breed resistance; resistance is growing. The thing grows in a spiral. It can only

> end one way. The excesses lead to resistance, resistance
> leads to brutality, the brutality leads to more resistance,
> and finally the question will be resolved with either the
> uneconomic destruction of the oppressed, or the end of
> oppression.

The chasm between Jackson's English and black vernacular could not be any greater.

The same rejection of the language of the street can be seen in the writings of the Black Panther Party chapter at San Quentin state prison in San Rafael, California. The February 27, 1971, edition of *The Black Panther* proudly published an article from the prison chapter, which is as gloomy prose as can be imagined:

> Now we realize that this pig has no laws which we as
> oppressed people are bound to respect. He cannot stifle
> our thoughts in order to slow up historical inevitable
> Revolution—Liberation. We say damn him and all his
> reactionary, fascist running dogs, because we will con-
> tinue to write and educate whenever we are among the
> masses and regardless of the repressive measure and re-
> percussion happening behind it.

Poor slang—it had no chance in the prison yard against the prison move-ment toughs with their Marxist jargon. So much for street slang as a badge of honor in the prison movement, bring on the rhetoric instead!

The Armed Forces

As students and anti-war activists mobilized against the war in Viet-nam, soldiers in active service as well as veterans built a movement that helped force the United States out of Vietnam. Beginning in 1967, the GI Movement, as it was called, hoped to break down the ability of the military to wage war in Vietnam. Hundreds of anti-war news-papers sprung from local GI organizations, and coffee houses opened near domestic army bases as safe havens for soldiers who opposed the war.

The GI movement deserted the Vietnam soldier's bright and expan-sive slang lexicon and instead drafted the jargon of social activism. Take, for example, John Kerry's statement on behalf of the Vietnam Veterans Against the War to the Senate Committee on Foreign Relations on April 23, 1971:

> In our opinion and from our experience, there is nothing in South Vietnam which could happen that realistically threatens the United States of America. And to attempt to justify the loss of one American life in Vietnam, Cambodia, or Laos by linking such loss to the preservation of freedom, which those misfits supposedly abuse, is to us the height of criminal hypocrisy, and it is that kind of hypocrisy which we feel has torn this country apart.

Or, take the rhetoric of GIs United Against the War in Vietnam, a successful organization made up mostly of African American and Latino soldiers at Fort Bragg and Fort Jackson:

> Meanwhile, our country suffers while the slaughter goes on. The vast resources and sums of money the government squanders in support of a corrupt dictatorship in Saigon belong to the Amerian people. It should be used to improve America, to make our country the shining example all of us want it to be—a free society—free of poverty and hunger, free of racial oppression, free of slums and illiteracy, and the misery they produce.

Given the language, it should come as no surprise that the Socialist Workers Party and their youth auxiliary the Young Socialist Alliance, were deeply involved in organizing GIs United Against the War in Vietnam.

Like others, soldiers checked their slang at the door when they began to organize active resistance to the war and the armed forces.

Gay Men

It is generally accepted that the genesis of political and social activism by American gays was what came to be known as the Stonewall riots in June 1969, when gay customers of the Stonewall Inn in Greenwich Village, New York, fought back police violence when the police raided the Inn, a favorite meeting place of homosexual men.

Shortly after the Stonewall raid and riots, activist groups arose and for the first time publicly resisted societal and legal oppression of homosexuals.

A month after Stonewall, flyers were distributed announcing the formation of an activist group to advance the cause of homosexuals. The flyer that was distributed in Greenwich Village to announce a meeting of what would become the Gay Liberation Front was bipolar, containing both hints of humor and slang and hints of the political rhetoric that was just around the corner:

DO YOU THINK HOMOSEXUALS ARE REVOLTING? YOU BET YOUR SWEET ASS WE ARE

We're going to make a place for ourselves in the revolutionary movement. We challenge the myths that are screwing up this society. MEETING: Thursday, July 24th, 6:30 PM at Alternate U, 69 West 14th Street at Sixth Avenue.

The Stonewall riots were led not by gentile, middle-class homosexuals, but by the most ostentatious and desperate in the fold, drag queens and boys basically living on the street. Because they are the element within the homosexual community most likely to use slang, it is not surprising that this initial call to arms contains both double meaning (revolting and sweet ass) and vernacular (you bet your sweet ass), as well as the dark clouds of political jargon ("the revolutionary movement").

A second leaflet, announcing the next meeting—in which the Gay Liberation Front was actually formed—had lost any hint of slang and had veered into the well-charted waters of political lingo.

HOMOSEXUALS ARE COMING TOGETHER AT LAST

"To examine how we are oppressed and how we oppress ourselves. To fight for gay control of gay businesses. To publish our own newspaper. To these and other radical ends. . . ."

At a third meeting, in August 1969, a seemingly inevitable 12-point manifesto was drafted and adopted without, it should be noted, any slang whatsoever:

A RADICAL MANIFESTO
THE HOMOPHILE MOVEMENT MUST
BE RADICALIZED!
(August 28, 1969)

l) We see the persecution of homosexuality as part of a general attempt to oppress all minorities and keep them powerless. Our fate is linked with these minorities; if the detention camps are filled tomorrow with blacks, hippies and other radicals, we will not escape that fate, all our attempts to dissociate ourselves from them notwithstanding. A common struggle, however, will bring common triumph.

2) Therefore we declare our support as homosexuals or bisexuals for the struggles of the black, the feminist, the Spanish American, the Indian, the Hippie, the Young, the Student, and other victims of oppression and prejudice.

3) We call upon these groups to lend us their support and encourage their presence with NACHO and the homophile movement at large.

4) Our enemies, an implacable, repressive governmental system; much of organized religion, business and medicine, will not be moved by appeasement or appeals to reason and justice, but only by power and force.

5) We regard established heterosexual standards of morality as immoral and refuse to condone them by demanding an equality which is merely the common yoke of sexual repression.

6) We declare that homosexuals, as individuals and members of the greater community, must develop homosexual ethics and esthetics independent of, and without reference to, the mores imposed upon heterosexuality.

7) We demand the removal of all restriction on sex between consenting persons of any sex, of any orientation, of any age, anywhere, whether for money or not, and for the removal of all censorship.

8) We call upon the churches to sanction homosexual liaisons when called upon to do so by the parties concerned.

9) We call upon the homophile movement to be more honestly concerned with youth rather than trying to promote a mythical, non-existent "good public image."

10) The homophile movement must totally reject the insane war in Viet Nam and refuse to encourage complicity in the war and support of the war machine, which may well be turned against us. We oppose any attempts by the movement to obtain security clearances for homosexuals, since these contribute to the war machine.

11) The homophile movement must engage in continuous political struggle on all fronts.

12) We must open the eyes of homosexuals on this continent to the increasingly repressive nature of our society and to the realizations that Chicago may await us tomorrow.

Once the Gay Liberation Front was formed, slang was forever lost as part of the language of activist gays. In 1972, Bruce Rodgers published *The Queens' Vernacular*, one of the finest and most vibrant slang dictionaries ever published on any subject. In his introduction, Rodgers acknowledged that politically active gay leaders had rejected the slang that he had so joyfully collected: "Many gay militants are avidly opposed to this contrived lingo with which the oppressed faggot makes himself understood, and then only to a 'sister.' They consider the jargon yet another link in the chain which holds the homosexual enslaved."

The Gay Liberation Front faded with the political activism of the 1970s, but political activism within the Gay, Lesbian, Bisexual and Transgender communities gained steam. No homosexual activist group was more politically charged than ACT-UP (the AIDS Coalition to Unleash Power), a radical activist AIDS group that advocated innovative, confrontational direct action on the AIDS issue. ACT-UP's glossary is only slightly more slangy than Roberts' Rules of Order with an endless litany of political terminology from "affinity group" to "caucus" to "direct action to outreach." Several slang terms survive (most notably **process queen** for someone who insists on strict adherence to the rules of order and **zap** for an action occurring within the upcoming week, but on the whole the language is dull, lackluster, and predictable.

Mexican American

Mexican-American vernacular English is filled with slang—pound for pound it is probably as intensely slang-laden as any vernacular, between English-language slang, Spanish-language slang, and blends of English and Spanish into slang. Following the footsteps of African Americans, Mexican Americans in the late 1960s turned to social activism to advance their civil and economic rights. With that turn, the slang that had helped with their everyday resistance gave way to the jargon of social activism, as shown by two examples.

First is the Plan of Delano, a document that became something of a mission statement for Cesar Chavez and his young union for farm workers as they marched from Delano north to Sacramento in the weeks before Easter, 1966. The Plan avoids Marxist dogma, but it also avoids any hint of slang:

> We shall Strike. We shall pursue the REVOLUTION we have proposed. We are sons of the Mexican Revolution, a revolution of the poor seeking bread and justice. Our revolution will not be armed, but we want the existing social order to dissolve, we want a new social order. We are poor, we are humble, and our only choices is to Strike in those ranchers where we are not treated with the respect we deserve as working men, where our rights as free and sovereign men are not recognized. We do not want the paternalism of the rancher; we do not want the contractor; we do not want charity at the price of our dignity. We want to be equal with all the working men in the nation; we want just wage, better working conditions, a decent future for our children. To those who oppose us, be they ranchers, police, politicians, or speculators, we say that we are going to continue fighting until we die, or we win.

The second document of Chicano social activism is "El Plan de Aztlan," which was adopted at the first National Chicano Youth Liberation Conference in 1969:

> El Plan Espiritual de Aztlan sets the theme that La Raza must use their nationalism as the key or common

denominator for mass mobilization and organization. Once we are committed to the idea and philosophy of El Plan de Aztlan, we can only conclude that social, economic, cultural, and political independence is the only road to total liberation from oppression, exploitation, and racism.

Some of this writing is better than the rest, but it is still strikingly slang-free. Once a group reaches the stage of issuing a manifesto or plan, you can be sure that they no longer need slang as a gesture of resistance.

The Exception to the Rule – Politicized Hippies

There is one interesting exception to the rule that the speech of the politically active is relatively slang-free, and that is the language of the political wing of the hippie movement of the late 1960s and early 1970s, which remained infused with slang. This dynamic is probably driven first and foremost by the nature of the oppression of hippies, but another factor was at work. When hippies acted politically, they were resisting not only the oppression of the dominant culture and power base, but also the intellectual and emotional oppression of the American left, and their language reflected that dual focus.

If there is a single document that exemplifies the thinking and language of the New Left, it would be the Port Huron Statement, the manifesto of the Students for a Democratic Society drafted in 1962 at an SDS convention in Port Huron, Michigan. The statement was a beacon of enlightenment and hope for a generation of social activists, yet it is entirely lacking in the fervor and passion of the generation for whom the SDS was trying to speak. The language is dense, intellectual, and academic throughout. Trying to work your way through this passage would leave the reader wondering how it could possibly have been written by young rebels: "The political order should serve to clarify problems in a way instrumental to their solution; it should provide outlets for the expression of personal grievance and aspiration; opposing views should be organized so as to illuminate choices and facilitate the attainment of goals; channels should be commonly available to relate men to knowledge and to power so that private problems—from bad recreation facilities to personal alienation—are formulated as general issues." There is no joy in this language, no spark, no slang.

While the hippie movement was largely apolitical and mutually un-aligned with the New Left, there was a political wing that bridged the gap between the drop-out-tune-out-turn-on ethic of hippies and the hardcore, take-no-prisoners political ethic of the New Left. The voice of this wing rejected the opaque political jargon of the New Left. As seen in the writings of Abbie Hoffman, Jerry Rubin, the Diggers, and John Sinclair, this voice embraced slang as not just the medium, but also as the message.

Abbie Hoffman, an unpredictable, tireless, social and political activist until his death in 1989, wrote in *Woodstock Nation* (1969) about an SDS conference and the dull, largely unfathomable language that the New Left was using: "Throughout the conference, I marveled at how little I understood what was being said. Songs like 'male chauvinism,' 'petit bourgeois revisionist,' 'puppet lackeys,' 'tool of the military-industrial complex,' and 'member of the proletariat vanguard waging the relentless battle against imperialism' were sung and other tunes that escape me for the moment. They are vibrations in another plastic dome. Going to that SDS conference was a bummer." [*Woodstock Nation* (1969) 54]. In this dismissal of political jargon, Hoffman resorted to hippie slang with "vibrations," "plastic," and "bummer."

Slang, not Marxist clichés, fills Hoffman's writing, as exemplified by these two short passages from *Woodstock Nation* (1969).

※ ※ ※

"Fuck the System" presents ways in which you help
take a free trip without working."
　　　—Abbie Hoffman: *Woodstock Nation* (1969) 113

So there I was organizing left-movement groups to
go to a hip community event—the Morea-Eel of the
Motherfuckers whose role I sometimes think is just to
chew me out, would be pissed and would be even if he
got a cut of the bread. Even if he got a cut of the bread
from this book he'd be pissed.
　　　—Abbie Hoffman: *Woodstock Nation* (1969) 128

Hoffman's co-conspirator in social activism, Jerry Rubin was militant, impulsive, dramatic, and creative. His 1970 political manifesto of hippie politics, *Do It!*, rings with slang:

❖ ❖ ❖

I dig department stores, huge supermarkets, and
airports. I feel secure (though not necessarily hungry)
when I see Howard Johnson's on the expressway. I
groove on Hollywood movies—even bad ones.
—Jerry Rubin: *Do It!* (1970) 12

Straights shit in their pants when they hear the yippies
reveal the most crucial political issue in Amerika today:
pay toilets.
—Jerry Rubin: *Do It!* (1970) 86

Get high and you want to turn on the world. It's never
"my dope"—it's always "our dope."
—Jerry Rubin: *Do It!* (1970) 98

San Francisco's Diggers were a group of radical improvisational actors who infused San Francisco's hippie scene with a streak of guerilla
theater. They considered themselves "community anarchists," and they
were decidedly political, especially in contrast to the generally apolitical/
apathetic/anti-political hippie ethos. The writings of Emmett Grogan,
the highest profile Digger, are slang-laced, as were the *Digger Papers*, a
free newspaper circulated by the Diggers in the summer of 1968, out-
lining their manifesto for what they called the Post-Competitive, Com-
parative Game of a Free City. While perhaps not as slangy as *The Oracle*
or other underground newspapers, the *Digger Papers* used the vernacular
with ease:

❖ ❖ ❖

nothing in these stores should be throwaway items . . .
space should be available for chicks to sew dresses,

make pants to order, recut garments to fit, etc. The
management should all be life-actors capable of turning
bullshitters into mud, important that these places
are first class environments with no trace of salvation
army/st. vinnie de paul charity rot. Everything groovy.
—*Digger Papers* (August 1968) 15

Even more extreme in his politics than Hoffman or Rubin or Grogan
and the Diggers, John Sinclair was the most visible leader of the White
Panther Party, a far-left, anti-racist political collective. While the White
Panthers were certainly capable of stultifyingly dull political language in
officials writings such as the "White Panther State/meant" of November
1968 with its ten-point program, Sinclair himself, though, wrote and
spoke the poetry of slang:

❉ ❉ ❉

Levine hassled the pigs until he was sure that subtle
persuasion wouldn't work (resulting in one cop pushing
Fred Smith in the chest and threatening him with a
whupping) and then returned to the club, turned on the
p.a., and informed the eager MC5 fans that me and
Dennis were getting popped in the parking lot and that
the only way they'd get to hear the band would be to
surround the cops outside and make them give us up.
—John Sinclair: *Guitar Army* (1972) 76

What accounts for the survival of slang in the language of the socially
active hippie? It may be as simple as the fact that the oppression felt by
hippies, socially active or not, was both temporary and voluntary. In *Do
It!*, Jerry Rubin argued that "Long hair turns white middle-class youth
into niggers" (94) and that hippies were "exploited and oppressed, and
we are fighting for *our freedom*." (115).

Perhaps Rubin believed this in the heat of the moment, but compared with those who were truly oppressed and had been for centuries,
the counterculture of the 1960s was more scorned than oppressed. The
lifestyle which earned them the disdain of the Establishment was one

which they embraced voluntarily and one which they could leave voluntarily whenever they wanted to. If it was long hair, as Rubin argued, that made hippies oppressed, a haircut was the instant ticket out of oppression.

As voluntary and short-term members of the oppressed class, hippies relied on the language of other groups, most prominently African Americans, for an instant *patois*. There were certainly terms and phrases that were coined by the young members of the hippie counterculture, yet most of their slang was borrowed, directly or indirectly through the beats and hipsters of the 1950s and early 1960s, from African-American vernacular English. Even when waxing political, the slang provided *bona fides*, reminding that white middle-class youth could be cool, hip, and—yes—oppressed.

This fact, then, as well as the fact that politicized hippies were revolting in part against the linguistic tyranny of the new American left's clichéd, impenetrable rhetoric, explains why slang not only survived, but flourished, in the language of political hippies.

The Lesbian Question

All lesbians are doubly oppressed, first as women and secondly as homosexuals, and lesbians of color are triply oppressed. Despite the scorn and discrimination endured by lesbians, their lexicon is not particularly slangy, making them an exception to the rule of oppression breeding slang.

This observation is neither original nor particularly new. The first serious consideration of homosexual slang in the United States was Gershon Legman's "The Language of Homosexuality" in George Henry's *Sex Variants* (1941). In the introduction to the glossary, Legman noted "the seeming absence of almost any but 'outsiders' slang in relation to female homosexuality" (1155). Legman offered three factors that he thought explained the absence of slang: (1) "The tradition of gentlemanly restraint among Lesbians stifles the flamboyance and conversational cynicism in sexual matters that slang coinage requires" (1156); (2) lesbianism is "a faddish vice among the intelligentsia" (1156); and (3) there is "greater tolerance in America toward Lesbians than toward homosexual men" (1156).

A very different point of view is found in Julia Penelope's *Sexist Slang and the Gay Community*, Michigan Occasional Papers in Women's Studies No. XIV (Summer 1979). Penelope joined Legman in observing that "Lesbians apparently do not possess a unique vocabulary that serves specific needs for the members of the group" (11). Her theory for why departs from Legman though—"Lesbians have been socially and historically invisible in our society and isolated from each other as a consequence, and have never had a cohesive community in which a lesbian aesthetic could have developed" (11–12).

Slang lexicographer Leonard Ashley has recorded and written on lesbian slang, and even as a champion of the language he concedes in "Dyke Diction: The Language of Lesbians" in *Maledicta* (1982), that lesbians "have more slang slung at them than they use" (135). Noting the role of separatist politics and politicolinguistics, Ashley observed that lesbians "are more likely to salt their speech with terms of the Lib movement than the lesbian subdivision of it and insofar as the Movement has estranged lesbians from their gay brothers it has reduced the gay component in women's slang" (136).

In her brilliant 1975 *Language and Woman's Place*, Robin Lakoff takes a broader view of the issue, analyzing women's speech. Many of her observations about women's speech are instructive as to the dearth of slang in lesbian language. Lakoff starts her politicolinguistic analysis with the general comment that "The social discrepancy in the positions of men and women in our society is reflected in the linguistic disparities" (46–47). From an early age, girls are socialized to speak differently than boys in several ways: (1) "Women's speech differs from men's in that women are more polite, which is precisely as it should be, since women are the preservers of morality and civility" (51); (2) "Women don't use off-color or indelicate expressions, women are the experts at euphemism" (55); and (3) "Hypercorrect forms and avoidance of colloquialism are another means of achieving distance" (65). To the extent that Lakoff is correct about women in general, her observations about women in general are applicable to lesbians and their language.

A final factor may help explain the paucity of slang in the lexicon of lesbian women in addition to those cited by Legman, Penelope, Ashley, and Lakoff. From the moment that lesbians came out from the shadows in the early 1970s and stepped into a cohesive community in which lesbian culture could develop, many have been closely linked with the women's movement. This involvement with an overtly political movement and its overtly political language would at least partially explain the serious nature of lesbian culture and language. If open resistance dulls the use of slang, a community that has been engaged in some level of open resistance since it became a community in the early 1970s would not be expected to be a rich source of slang. As Ashley noted, the language of separatist politics is more easily found than slang in the language of lesbians.

CHAPTER 8

Conclusion

If someone who knew nothing about American culture were to study the United States today, they would quickly observe that the loudest voices raging against their oppression would be a curious collection of media figures—Sarah Palin, Carrie Prejean, Rush Limbaugh, Bill O'Reilly, Glenn Beck, and Sean Hannity. Daily and incessantly they chronicle their oppression and the oppression of their audiences by forces described in sometimes contradictory and mutually exclusive terminology.

And—the observer would hear precious little slang from these new self-proclaimed spokespersons of the oppressed, despite their ubiquitous media presence and the staggering amount of words they share with the public every day. Seriously though, this seemingly privileged group is oppressed? Not so much. Of course, the rightwing pretenders to the crown of oppression are *not* oppressed and almost certainly they don't truly believe that they are oppressed, even if their followers might see themselves and their icons as oppressed and persecuted. The public figures claiming oppression are white, wealthy, firmly aligned with global corporate interests, Christian, and several (most notably Palin and Prejean) who wear their sometimes confusing theology on their sleeves are quick to play the religious card when criticized, with or without a rational nexus to their religious beliefs.

These (wink, wink) oppressed use little slang for the simple reason that they are The Man, they always were The Man and always will be The Man. In usurping the mantle of oppression, they are engaging in the ultimate exploitation of the oppressed. The oppressed, having had their expressive culture (fashion, music, graphic arts, and slang to name a few) long since mimicked and outright stolen by the dominant culture, are now faced with having their very claim to oppression lifted by not just the mainstream culture, but by the faces and voices of the very oppressor, the Man. First the trappings, and now the crown, now the title. The spokesmen and spokesgal and spokes-dethroned-queen of fauxpression have, in the words of Greg Tate, taken everything but the burden from the oppressed.

Rightists in general use little slang and are profoundly out of touch with slang, so much so that the loosely knit band of zealots heeding the call of the fire-breathers and protesting all-things-Obama in 2009 used the term "teabag" to describe a protest tactic in which they mailed teabags to President Obama as a reminder of the Boston Tea Party. The original "teabag" verbers were apparently blissfully unaware of the sexual slang meaning of the term. Liberal bloggers and commentators pounced on the right's use of a word understood in some circles to mean sucking a man's scrotum, leading the right to charge back with cries of juvenile humor not suitable to the high level of political discourse displayed by the protestors with their Obama as witch doctor and Obama as Hitler placards. This brief, inadvertent excursion into sexual slang is the only demonstrable use of slang by the rightwing pretenders to the throne of oppression, although slang terms and phrases are often attached to several of them—the term "boob job" is often mentioned in conjunction with Carrie Prejean because of her surgically enlarged breasts, and "drug-addled gasbag" is often mentioned in conjunction with Rush Limbaugh (as a result of his quite public addiction to synthetic opiates).

No, those most loudly and vociferously claiming oppression are fiercely loyal to the existing order in which they and fellow wealthy, corporate-aligned, white Christians conduct the affairs of society and state. If anything, their instinct would be to mock and otherwise repress slang, just as they mock and repress all challenges to the existing state of affairs. To claim oppression and to be oppressed are not necessarily one and the same. To be criticized for hypocrisy or to have one's views challenged is neither oppression nor persecution, it is the price one pays for venturing into the public arena with strong opinions and judgments of others. Whatever it may be, the Palin-Limbaugh axis is not oppressed, and their failure to use slang should not be surprising.

Further left on the radio dial, the observer would note occasional sharp protestations of oppression by the Rev. Jesse Jackson and the Rev. Al Sharpton, the go-to subject matter experts when a race-tinged incident has taken place. Their rhetoric is not exactly standard political rhetoric and the influences of the Black preacher tradition are apparent in the speech of both men, but the use of African-American vernacular is slim to none in their public speech.

Again, this should not be surprising, for three reasons. For one, we know that the oppressed tend to drop slang as a weapon of resistance when they graduate from everyday resistance to open and notorious resistance, and both Jackson and Sharpton have spent their lives openly resisting racial oppression. Secondly, slang is often class-based, and both men have unabashed aspirations to at least middle-class status. Those who pursue bourgeois standing commonly embrace bourgeois values, including middle-class linguistic norms. Lastly, their religious backgrounds gave these men a rhetorical foundation other than street slang and left them less inclined than others to borrow from the sometimes frantic language of the streets.

To find the use of slang as everyday resistance today, don't look to the privileged voices of the right and don't look to the leaders of minority groups—look to the ghetto, the *shtetl*, the *barrio*, the barracks, or prison, both as a physical location and as a notional community. Oppression in the United States today for the most part pales in comparison to historic oppression here or contemporary oppression elsewhere, yet it is nevertheless oppression, and even diminished instances may resonate in a magnified manner with past severe oppression.

Those who are the object of oppression in the United States still respond to oppression exactly as one would expect, either with obsequious embrace of the oppressor or by following the precepts of Tacitus and acting on the natural desire to resist oppression. Overt collective defiance is rarer than it ever has been, yet small acts of everyday resistance are still common—passive aggression, disguised circumvention of power, acts of public anonymity undermining authority, dishonesty and vandalism, and expressive culture all serve to subvert the existing order.

By its very nature, slang continues to be subversive. Besides the meaning conveyed by the slang term or phrase, its mere usage signals a group membership and conjures tribal loyalty, especially when the "tribe" or group using the slang is an outsider group. Slang's rejection of standard and conventional English is subversive in and of itself—perhaps mildly so, but subversive nonetheless because it implicitly challenges the established social order, the *status quo*, and conventional norms.

When used as a means of everyday resistance, slang becomes twice subversive. It is not just a rejection of linguistic norms, it is a rejection of the *status quo* in all respects, a blow against the empire, another brick from the wall. Slang used as everyday resistance is a symbol of potential revolution against convention and the established social order. The oppressed still use slang to build a collective identity with shared values, and with slang they show respect for each other which is otherwise absent in public life. Their slang ridicules and shows contempt for their oppressor and especially for those in their class who side with the oppressor. Humor and strong words still ring within the slang of the oppressed.

Slang as used by the oppressed turns the world upside down. If the world that is supposed to be good is seen by the oppressed as harsh, uncaring, and unjust, then it is no surprise that in the counter-narrative of the oppressed good is bad and bad is good. If racial, economic, religious, or sexual persecution is acceptable, then inversion is a rational and understandable response.

The book of *Matthew* attributes to Jesus Christ the somewhat pessimistic view that the poor will always be with us. Where there are poor, Tacitus tells us that there is resistance, and here we have seen that where there is resistance, among that resistance is slang. By the distributive law of mathematics, slang as resistance thus will always be with us. Right on!

Index